KAUAI

HOW TO USE THIS GUIDEBOOK

This guidebook is divided into four sections: *An Introduction to Kauai, The History of Kauai, Kauai* and *Ni'ihau.*

The first two sections comprise essays designed to provide you with facts on the area.

In the next two sections, we explore Kauai and Ni'ihau, with a detailed geographic breakdown of the area. Each section contains descriptions of the various places and points of interest, followed by a sebsection entitled *Practical Information.* The *Practical Information* is designed to provide you with a ready reference to accommodations, restaurants, places of interest, beaches, seasonal events, recreation, tours, etc., with hours, prices, addresses and phone numbers.

A quick and easy way into this book is the *Index* at the end.

California Series

The Complete Gold Country Guidebook
The Complete Lake Tahoe Guidebook
The Complete Monterey Peninsula Guidebook
The Complete San Diego Guidebook
The Complete Wine Country Guidebook
Vacation Towns of California

Hawaii Series

The Complete Kauai Guidebook
The Complete Maui Guidebook
The Complete Oahu Guidebook
The Complete Big Island of Hawaii Guidebook

Mexico Series

The Complete Baja California Guidebook
The Complete Yucatan Peninsula Guidebook

Caribbean Series

The Complete Virgin Islands Guidebook
The Complete Jamaica Guidebook
The Complete Puerto Rico Guidebook

Indian Chief Travel Guides are available from your local bookstore or Indian Chief Publishing House, P.O. Box 1814, Davis, CA 95617.

The Complete
KAUAI
Guidebook

Published by Indian Chief Publishing House
Davis, California

Text and Research: **DAVID J. RUSS**
Editor: **B. SANGWAN**
Photographs: **Davis Russ, John Hunt,**
    Princeville/Mojo
Cover Art and Maps: **B. Sangwan**

ISBN 0-916841-52-9

Printed in the U.S.A.

CONTENTS

HAWAIIAN ISLANDS

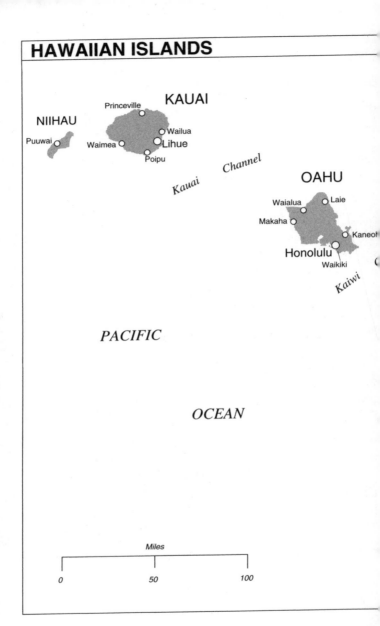

KAUAI

Princeville

NIIHAU

Puuwai

Waimea

Wailua

Lihue

Poipu

Kauai Channel

OAHU

Waialua

Laie

Makaha

Kaneohe

Honolulu

Waikiki

Kaiwi

PACIFIC

OCEAN

Miles

0   50   100

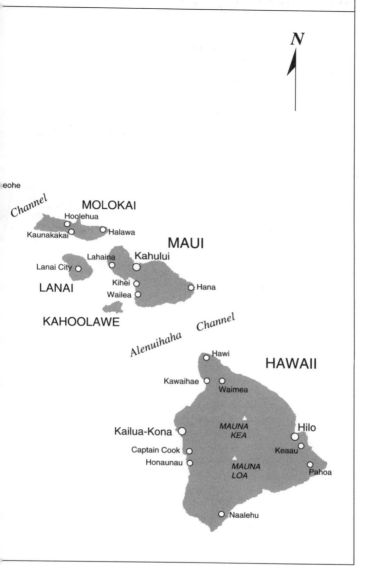

N

eohe

Channel

MOLOKAI

Hoolehua

Kaunakakai　　　Halawa

MAUI

Lahaina　　Kahului

Lanai City

LANAI

Kihei　　　　　　Hana

Wailea

KAHOOLAWE

Alenuihaha Channel

Hawi

HAWAII

Kawaihae　　Waimea

Kailua-Kona　　　　*MAUNA KEA*　　　Hilo

Captain Cook　　　　　　　　Keaau

Honaunau　　*MAUNA LOA*　　Pahoa

Naalehu

KAUAI AND NI'IHAU

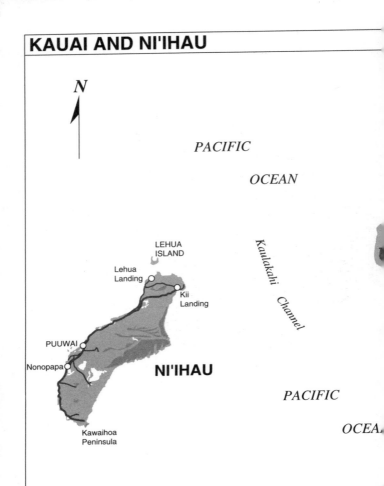

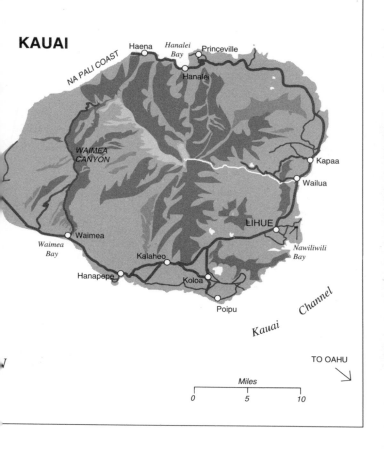

KAUAI

NA PALI COAST

Haena
Hanalei Bay
Princeville
Hanalei

WAIMEA CANYON

Kapaa
Wailua

LIHUE

Waimea

Waimea Bay

Kalaheo

Nawiliwili Bay

Hanapepe
Koloa

Poipu

Kauai *Channel*

W

TO OAHU

Miles

0   5   10

BULLETIN

On September 11, 1992, Kauai was struck by Hurricane Iniki, and several hotels, resorts, businesses and homes suffered major damage. However, the island has largely recovered since, with most of the hotels, restaurants, shops and other businesses now open, welcoming visitors once again.

Nearly all the establishments listed in this book are in business, although some may be temporarily closed for repairs or rebuilding. It is, therefore, recommended that visitors to Kauai call the respective establishments before visiting. Visitors may also call the toll-free KAUAI HOTLINE, at 1-800-262-1400, for the most current information on the island's hotels, restaurants, tour operators and other visitor facilities; the hotline is open 7 days a week, 6 a.m.-6 p.m. (Hawaiian Standard Time).

AN INTRODUCTION TO KAUAI

"Eden of Hawaii"

Kauai is the Eden of Hawaii, its "Garden Isle." It is rich in natural beauty, with unspoiled, lush rain forests, tropical gardens overflowing with color, ancient coconut groves, dramatic, mist-covered mountains plunging into the ocean, and miles upon miles of untouched, white-sand beaches, where few, if any, ever venture. It is, indeed, Hawaii's most beautiful, relatively undis-covered island.

Kauai is approximately 558 square miles in area — the fourth largest of the Hawaiian islands — with a population of around 52,000. It is also the northernmost of Hawaii's main islands, situated some 95 miles northwest of Oahu, with Ni'ihau, the small, mystery-laden island, just to the west of it. On Kauai itself, the rugged, picturesque Na Pali Coast makes up the northwest shore, with the Waimea Canyon — the "Grand Can-yon of the Pacific" — on the western part of the island, Poipu Beach on the south shore, and Princeville, a world-class resort area, on the north shore. The island's principal town is Lihue, situated on the southeast corner of the island.

Nearly 1.5 million tourists visit Kauai each year, mostly to enjoy the island's scenic and natural beauty and wealth of outdoor activities — typically, swimming, surfing, windsurfing, snorkeling, scuba diving, beachcombing, hiking, horseback riding, helicopter touring, and, in season, whale watching. Kauai also has over 7,000 hotel rooms and condominium accommodations, more than a hundred restaurants, and a temperate, yet supremely varied climate, ranging from around 60° in January to 85° or so in August.

Indeed, Kauai is Hawaii's most treasured destination resort — at once the oldest and the newest — and its best-kept secret.

THE HISTORY OF KAUAI

Kauai is Hawaii's oldest island. It began forming nearly 10 million years ago — the result of a series of eruptions on the ocean floor that created a single, shielded volcano, which, with the accumulation of molten lava over a period of time, finally emerged from the ocean as Mount Wai'ale'ale, some 5,148 feet above sea level, at the center of the island. Then, approximately a million years ago, Mount Waiale'ale became extinct, and in the following years, rivers, streams, ocean waves and the wind sculpted and shaped the island, with its valleys, canyons, cliffs and mountain ranges, notable among them the ancient, deeply eroded Waimea Canyon and the stunning sea cliffs along the Na Pali Coast.

An ancient Hawaiian myth, however, endures that Kauai and the other Hawaiian islands are the offspring of Wakea, the divine embodiment of the sky, and Papa, the earth deity, who arrived in this part of the Pacific from Tahiti. Wakea and Papa first conceived Hawaii, the big island, followed by Maui. Wakea then conceived with Kaulawahine — another deity — the island of Lanai, and with Hina, the island of Molokai. Papa, for her part, thoroughly infuriated, conceived with Lua — a male deity —

the island of Oahu. Finally, with all that accomplished, Wakea and Papa reconciled and together conceived Kauai — the most noble of the islands, "born of heavenly quality" — as well as the nearby island of Ni'ihau and its adjoining islets, Lehua and Kaula.

Kauai was also the first Hawaiian island to be inhabited. Its earliest inhabitants were the Marquesans, a Polynesian people who journeyed to Kauai from the Marquesas and Society islands between 500 A.D. and 750 A.D., followed, some years later, around 1000 A.D., by the Tahitians. The Marquesans, who journeyed to Hawaii in large outrigger canoes, navigating by the stars as they traveled across several thousand miles of open ocean, introduced to Kauai and the other Hawaiian islands the first domestic animals, plants and fruit; and the Tahitians, for their part, brought with them their religion, their gods and goddesses, notable among them — Kane, the god of all living creatures; Ku, god of war; Pele, goddess of fire; Kaneloa, the god of the land of the departed spirits; and Lono, god of harvest and peace. The Tahitians also introduced to the islands the *kapu* system, a strict social order that affected all aspects of life, and became the core of ancient Hawaiian culture.

According to legend, however, the island's first settlers were the *menehune*, Kauai's mysterious little people, pixie-like, and around 2-feet tall, who are credited with several engineering marvels around the island — such as the Menehune Ditch and Alakoko Fishpond — unique in their architecture, with inter-locking flanged and fitted cut-stone bricks. The *menehune* worked only at night, completing entire projects in the course of a single night, and their strength was in their numbers — there were so many *menehune*, according to popular belief, that they could form two rows from Makaweli to Wailua (nearly 30 miles distant). The *menehune*, nevertheless, left Kauai just as myste-riously as they had arrived — although, in a recent census, some 53 Hawaiians claimed to be descendants of the *menehune*.

The first white man to arrive in Kauai was Captain James Cook, a British explorer in search of a northwest passage from the Pacific Ocean to the Atlantic Ocean. He landed at Waimea, on Kauai's west shore, on January 20, 1778; it was his first landing in the Hawaiian islands. In the following years, others followed, including Nathaniel Portlock and George Dixon, who had served under Cook, and Captain George Vancouver, another British explorer, who also landed at Waimea, in March of 1792. These early Europeans, however, also brought with them to Kauai and the other Hawaiian islands the white man's disease. The Hawaiians, of course, had little or no resistance to Western diseases, and over a period of some 100 years following Cook's first visit to the islands, nearly 80% of the indigenous Hawaiian population was wiped out.

The mid and late 1700s also ushered in Hawaii's era of monarchy. Kamehameha I — or Kamehameha the Great — was born in the late 1750s, and by 1791 he had gained control of the island of Hawaii, followed in 1794 — in his bid to bring all the Hawaiian islands under his rule — by the conquests of the nearby islands of Maui, Molokai and Lanai. In 1795, Kamehameha also conquered Oahu. His bid to conquer Kauai, however, was thwarted on at least two occasions, in 1796, by bad weather and turbulent seas, resulting in his failure to cross the Kauai Channel with his armada. Finally, in 1819, after learning of yet another attempt by Kamehameha to invade Kauai, King Kaumuali'i of Kauai, who had become the ruler of Kauai in 1796, at the age of 16, ceded the island to Kamehameha. Kauai, thus, became a tributary kingdom of Kamehameha the Great, even as Kaumuali'i was permitted to continue to govern the island.

In the early 1800s, too, the first Russians arrived in Kauai: a ship owned by the Russian American Company, an agent of the Russian government, engaged in the fur trade, ran aground just off the southwest coast of Kauai; and in 1816, Georg Scheffer, a German in the service of the Russian company, was sent to secure the goods of the ship. Scheffer, however, once ashore, built, at the mouth of the Waimea River — near the settlement of Waimea — a Russian fort, and named it Fort Elizabeth, for Czarina Elizabeth, wife of Alexander I. The Russian presence on the island, nevertheless, was short-lived, and the fort was soon abandoned by Scheffer.

The 1820s brought the first missionaries to the Hawaiian islands. The earliest missionaries on Kauai were Samuel and Mercy Whitney, who arrived at Waimea in 1820, to establish a mission. The Whitneys were followed by others: in 1828, Peter Gulick arrived in Waimea, and some years later, in 1835, established the Koloa Mission in nearby Koloa; in 1834, William Alexander journeyed to Hanalei, on Kauai's north shore, and established the Waioli Mission; and in 1841, Father Walsh, a Catholic priest, established the first Catholic mission in Koloa, then went on to build, in 1856, the nearby St. Raphael's Church. Among other notable early-day missionaries were George Rowell, who arrived in Waimea in 1846, and built there the Gulick House, the Great Stone Church and the Waimea Hawaiian Church; and Abner and Lucy Wilcox, who lived and worked at the mission in Hanalei in the late 1800s.

The year 1835 witnessed the birth of Hawaii's sugar industry — at Koloa, on Kauai's south shore. The first sugar plantation and mill were established at Koloa that year, by William Hooper of Ladd & Company of Honolulu. Other sugarcane plantations followed, at Lihue in 1849, at the Grove Farm, near Lihue, in 1864, and at Kekaha in 1898; and sugar became the island's principal industry for the next nearly 150 years, until it was finally displaced by tourism. A vestige of Kauai's sugar industry, however, the old Lihue Sugar Mill, built in 1849, is still in operation, processing more than 65,000 tons of raw sugar annually.

The late 1800s and early 1900s also brought to the Hawaiian islands waves of immigrants — mostly Chinese, Japanese, Filipino, Portuguese and other Europeans — drawn to Hawaii's growing sugar and pineapple industries. The numbers of these new immigrants, of course, over time, turned Hawaii's indigenous population into a minority. On Kauai, in fact, Filipinos now comprise 27% of the population, Japanese 26%, caucasians 22%, mixed-blood Hawaiians 18%, and pure-blooded, native Hawaiians only 2%.

In the late 1800s also, after the death of Kamehameha V, Hawaiian monarchy fell into disarray, and the custom of electing a king was established. At about this time, too, with the growth of Hawaii's sugar industry, American interests on the island increased. In 1892, upon the start of open rebellion, the *U.S.S. Boston* landed on the island of Oahu an armed force to protect American interests; and a year later, in 1893, the more or less bloodless revolution brought to power, at the head of a provisional government, Sanford B. Dole. The following year, Hawaii was declared a republic by the Hawaiian legislature, and on June 14, 1900, Hawaii was annexed, under the Organic Act, by the United States, and a territorial form of government established.

In 1902, Prince Jonah Kuhio Kalanianaole, born on Kauai, of royal parentage, and the last heir to the throne, became the first Hawaiian delegate elected to the U.S. Congress. Kuhio led the Hawaiian congressional delegation for the next two decades, and despite not having an official vote in the legislature — as Hawaii was only a territory of the United States at the time — he forged important legislation for the betterment of Hawaii and its people, including the landmark Hawaiian Homesteads Act of 1910 and the Hawaiian Homes Commission Act of 1921, whereby public lands were made available to native Hawaiians for homesteading. He also obtained funding for such important projects as Nawiliwili, Kauai's only deep-water port, and Pearl Harbor and Kahului Harbor; and in 1919 and 1920, he introduced the first two successive bills for statehood for Hawaii in the House of Representatives. In 1922, however, Kuhio died, at the age of 50.

On August 21, 1959, Hawaii finally gained statehood, becoming the 50th state of the nation — the "Aloha State." That same year, the first commercial jet, a Boeing 707, landed in the islands, at Honolulu, greatly reducing travel time from the continental U.S. to Hawaii, to under $4\frac{1}{2}$ hours. This, effectively, signalled the beginning of tourism in Hawaii.

In the following decade, Hawaii's tourist era began in earnest. On the island of Kauai, the Coco Palms Hotel, the island's first tourist hotel, which had originally been built as a 12-room hotel in 1953, expanded into a full-fledged, 390-room establishment in the 1960s. Also in the 1960s, Poipu Beach began to develop into a premier resort, beginning with the construction of the Waiohai Hotel — forerunner of the Waiohai Beach Resort — in the early 1960s and the Sheraton Kauai a few years later. In 1970, development began on the multi-million-dollar Princeville Resort — which included two golf courses, a shopping center and a small, commercial airport — and in the late 1970s the first Holiday Inn opened on Kauai's east shore, near Wailua. In the 1980s, of course, yet more resort hotels sprang up on the island's south and east shores, including the Kauai Hilton, Kauai Beach Boy, Stouffer's, and, the grandest of all, the $350-million Westin Kauai.

In August, 1972, on Kauai, even as resort development continued unabated, the Palm Tree Ordinance was passed, to minimize the impact of it all on the island and its inhabitants. The ordinance, effectively, restricted the height of all new buildings on the island to approximately that of a palm tree — 40 feet or four stories. The tallest building on the island is now the Westin Kauai, 10 stories high, originally built in 1959.

The 1950s, 60s, 70s and 80s also witnessed the creation of a series of state parks and sanctuaries — among them the Waimea Canyon and Kokee state parks, originally established in 1952; the Na Pali Coast State Park, encompassing 6,175 acres, established in 1962; the Haena State Park on Kauai's north shore and 917-acre Hanalei Valley Wildlife Refuge, established in 1972; and the Kilauea Point National Wildlife Refuge, with 160 acres set aside for endangered seabirds, established in 1988.

On November 23, 1982, however, Kauai suffered one of its its worst setbacks, when Hurricane Iwa, with winds of nearly 95 m.p.h. and waves breaking at heights of over 30 feet, devastated the island's south and west shores, destroying both resort and residential communities in the area, causing damage in excess of $200 million. And again, on September 11, 1992, Kauai bore the brunt of the single worst natural disaster in its history. Hurricane Iniki struck the island in all its fury, with sustained winds of 130 m.p.h. and gales up to 160 m.p.h. More than 7,000 homes were razed, leaving thousands of islanders homeless, most hotels and resorts suffered severe damage, virtually all the island's sugarcane and macadamia nut crop was lost, and the telephone, power and water systems failed. The hurricane left in its wake damage estimated at nearly $2 billion.

Kauai, nevertheless, has largely recovered, and is now, once again, positioned as a premier destination resort, with an abundance of excellent hotel and condominium accommodations and restaurants and other visitor facilities, and a wealth of recreational opportunities, including swimming, snorkeling, scuba diving, surfing, windsurfing, sailing, fishing, hiking, camping, horseback riding, beachcombing, helicopter touring, tennis, golf, and more.

KAUAI

"The Garden Isle"

Kauai is Hawaii's "Garden Isle." And with good reason. It is the most beautiful of the Hawaiian islands, with verdant valleys dotted with countless waterfalls and criss-crossed by rivers and streams, and tropical gardens overflowing with lush plants and flowers and a bounty of stunning color. It has some of the loveliest, untouched beaches — from Poipu to Polihale, Lumahai, Ke'e and even Kalalau — and a spectacular coastline along its northwestern end. It also has on it the wettest spot on earth, Mount Wai'ale'ale, and the picturesque, pine-clad Kokee State Park and famous Waimea Canyon, the "Grand Canyon of the Pacific."

Kauai is approximately 558 square miles in area, the fourth largest of the Hawaiian islands — and the northernmost. It is also the oldest of the Hawaiian islands, and rich in legends and lore. Its chief areas of interest include — Lihue, the principal town, situated on the southeastern corner of the island; the South Shore, with sunny Poipu Beach and the historic town of Koloa; the West Side, which includes the scenic Waimea Canyon and Kokee State Park and secluded Polihale Beach; the East Side, which has in it the all-important Wailua River and the towns of Wailua and Kapa'a; and the North Shore, which takes in the towns of Kilauea and Hanalei, Princeville Resort, and the fabled Lumahai Beach and Na Pali Coast.

Kauai is situated some 95 miles northwest of Oahu, with the tiny island of Ni'ihau 17 miles or so to the west of it. It can be reached by air, on inter-island flights, from Honolulu, Oahu. The island's main airport, the Lihue Airport, is located in Lihue, with a smaller, commuter airport located at Princeville, on Kauai's north shore.

KAUAI

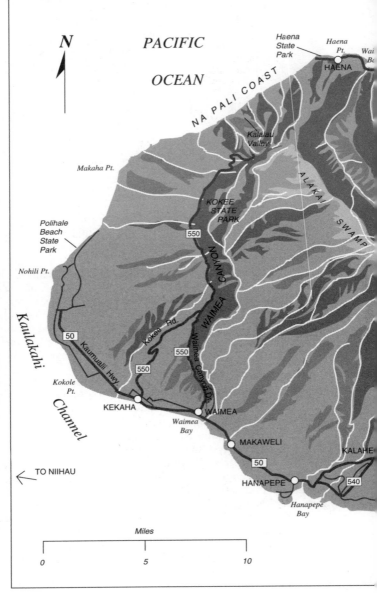

N

PACIFIC

OCEAN

Haena
State
Park

Haena
Pt.

Wai
Be

HAENA

NA PALI COAST

Kalalau
Valley

Makaha Pt.

KOKEE
STATE
PARK

ALAKAI SWAMP

Polihale
Beach
State
Park

550

Nohili Pt.

WAIMEA CANYON

Kokee Rd.

Waimea Canyon Dr.

Kaulakahi

50

Kaumualii Hwy.

550

550

Kokole
Pt.

550

KEKAHA

WAIMEA

Channel

Waimea
Bay

MAKAWELI

KALAHE

← TO NIIHAU

50

HANAPEPE

540

Hanapepe
Bay

Miles

0   5   10

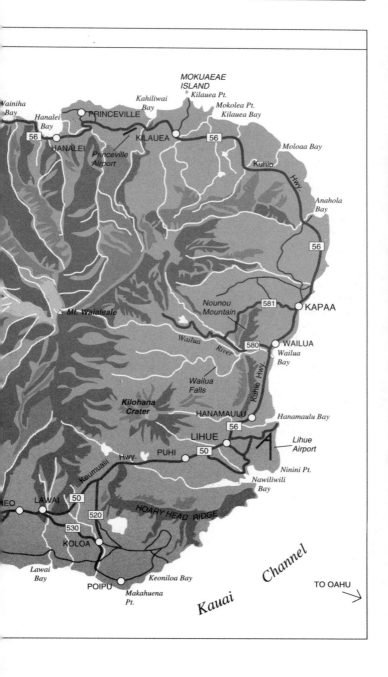

THE LIHUE AREA

Lihue

The best, or, perhaps, the most convenient place to begin your tour of Kauai, we might suggest, is Lihue, a small, urban center, situated on the southeast corner of the island, more or less equidistant from the east and north shores and the south and west shores — the two areas of visitor interest, which, by the way, are cut off from each other at the northwest end of the island by the rugged and virtually inaccessible Na Pali Coast. Lihue also, we might add, is the commercial and civic center of Kauai (and the nearby island of Ni'ihau), and it has in it, besides, Kauai's main airport, the Lihue Airport — which handles most of the island's commercial flights — as well as the island's principal port, Nawiliwili, situated just to the south of the center of town, where most of the cruise ships and freighters bound for Kauai call.

The Lihue township itself, however, in all fairness, is rather uninspiring, but it does have a few places of visitor interest in and around it. Here, for instance, in the center of town, on Rice Street — the town's main street — you can search out a handful of 1930s buildings, most notably the old County Building, the Bank of Hawaii Building, and the two-story A.S. Wilcox Memorial Library Building which now houses the well-regarded Kauai Museum, where displays, typically, are centered on the history of Kauai — the oldest of the Hawaiian Islands — from the geological origins of the island to present day, with several excellent exhibits, including scores of artifacts and old photographs and films depicting the "Story of Kauai." There is also an art gallery on the premises, displaying works of local artists, and a gift shop with souvenirs and books of local interest.

Just to the south of the center of town also, on Rice Street and Kapena Road, at the very bottom, lies the sun-drenched, crescent-shaped white-sand Kalapaki Beach, situated at the head of Nawiliwili Bay — Kauai's only deep-water harbor, built in the 1930s, and where, on any given day, you can see scores of tug boats, fishing boats, sailing boats and other pleasure craft, and, often enough, cruise ships, containers ships, and even U.S. naval vessels. Kalapaki Beach, by the way, has excellent swimming, surfing and sailing possibilities, and a little way from the beach, at the northeastern corner of Nawiliwili Bay, you can visit Ninini Point, an excellent place for whale watching, in season, that is.

At Kalapaki Beach, too, at its western end, is the rambling Kauai Marriott resort hotel, a dazzling, $350 million extravaganza, originally developed, in 1987, by Chris Hemmeter, Hawaii's most celebrated resort developer, whose triumphs include the Westin Maui, Hyatt Regency Maui, Hyatt Regency Waikiki and the Hyatt Regency Waikoloa. In any case, the Kauai Marriott consists of five multi-storied buildings — 3 to 10 stories high — with 335 rooms and suites and over 200 luxury time-share units, 6 restaurants, two shopping villages with some 30 well-stocked shops and boutiques, a mosaic-tiled, 26,000-square-foot swimming pool — one of the largest in Hawaii! — tennis courts, stables — with more than 100 thoroughbred horses, including Clydesdales, Percherons and Belgians — a 2-acre reflecting pond, and lagoons and islands in a 50-acre man-made lake, where gondoliers whisk visitors about in canopy-covered out-rigger canoes. There are also two 18-hole, championship golf courses here, the Kauai Lagoons Course and Kiele Course, designed by Jack Nicklaus. The Kauai Marriott, by the way, is linked to the Lihue Airport by a private, 2-mile-long road, owned by the resort.

Close at hand, and also of interest, is the Alakoko Fishpond Lookout, overlooking the ancient Alakoko Fishpond — also known as the Menehune Fishpond — located on Hulemalu Road, just to the west of Nawiliwili Harbor, and reached by way of Rice Street south and Nawiliwili Road (58) and Wilcox Road west and southwest, respectively, to Wa'apa Road, which, in turn, leads directly west to Hulemalu Road, and so to the lookout. The fishpond, however, is believed to have been built by Kauai's legendary little people, the *menehune*, who, we are told, carried the stones for the construction of the pond from Makaweli, some 25 miles distant, passing them hand to hand, down a double row of workers. The fishpond is located on the Hule'ia River — featured in the opening scenes of the *Raiders of the Lost Ark* — with walls that are 5 feet high and 100 feet long, rising above the water. It was built, according to popular belief, at the request of a princess and her brother, who promised not to watch the *menehune* as they worked, but, out of curiosity, did, and were thus turned to stone.

Another place of supreme interest, situated on Nawiliwili Road (58) — a mile or so southeastward from the intersection of Kaumuali'i Highway (50), or one and one-half miles northwest from Nawiliwili Harbor — is the Grove Farm Homestead, an authentic, 80-acre plantation-era estate, which has in it some of the island's oldest plantation homes and buildings, nestled amid orchards, vegetable gardens and cattle pastures. The Grove Farm was originally established by pioneer plantation owner George N. Wilcox in 1864, and has been wonderfully preserved, in its original state, with period furnishings and fixtures and even personal items, all left more or less untouched — suspended in time — reflective of a bygone era. Guided tours are

LIHUE

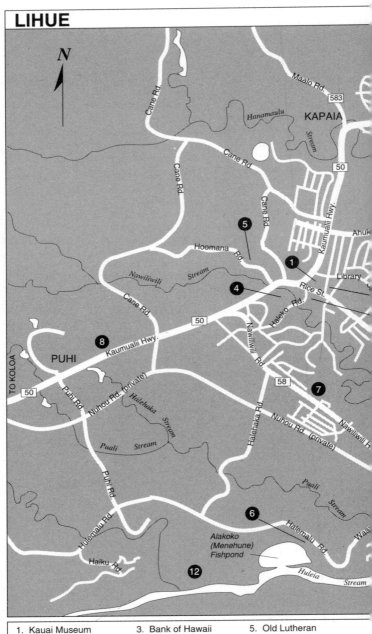

1. Kauai Museum
   (Wilcox Memorial
   Library Building)
2. County Building
3. Bank of Hawaii
   Building
4. Lihue Sugar Mill
   (1849)
5. Old Lutheran
   Church (1883)
6. Alakoko Fishpond
   Lookout

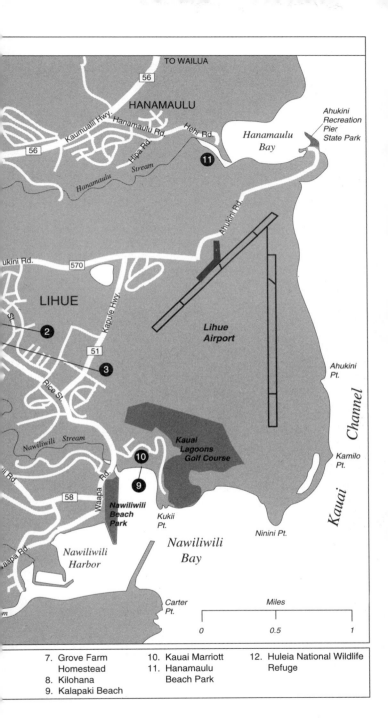

TO WAILUA

56

HANAMAULU

Kaumualii Hwy.   Hanamaulu Rd.   Hehi Rd.

Hanamaulu Bay

Ahukini Recreation Pier State Park

56

Hipa Rd.

Hanamaulu Stream

🅫

Ahukini Rd.

ukini Rd.   570

LIHUE

2

Kapule Hwy.

51

3

Rice St.

St.

Nawiliwili Stream

ili Rd.

58

Waapa Rd.

Kauai Marriott Waapa Rd.

10

9

Nawiliwili Beach Park

Nawiliwili Harbor

Nawiliwili

Kukii Pt.

Lihue Airport

Kauai Lagoons Golf Course

Ahukini Pt.

Kamilo Pt.

Ninini Pt.

Nawiliwili Bay

Kauai Channel

Carter Pt.

Miles

0   0.5   1

---

7. Grove Farm
   Homestead
8. Kilohana
9. Kalapaki Beach

10. Kauai Marriott
11. Hanamaulu
    Beach Park

12. Huleia National Wildlife
    Refuge

offered, by reservation, of both the buildings — including the main plantation home and the cottages and smaller workers' camp houses — as well as the grounds.

Also of interest, northwest from the Grove Farm Homestead a mile or so on Nawiliwili Road (58) to the Kaumuali'i Highway (50), and eastward a little way on the Kaumuali'i Highway — just west of the intersection of the Kaumuali'i and Kuhio highways — is the old Lihue Sugar Mill, originally built in 1849, when sugar was Kauai's principal industry, and Lihue was at the center of that growing industry. The Lihue Sugar Mill, still in operation, now processes an estimated 65,000 tons of sugar annually.

Nearby, too, just to the northwest from the sugar mill, on Hoomana Road, which goes off the Kaumuali'i Highway, stands the Old Lutheran Church, built in 1883 to service the large German population in the area at the time, and claimed to be oldest Lutheran church in Hawaii.

North of Lihue, of course, and also worth visiting, is the Hanama'ulu Beach Park, situated at the head of Hanama'ulu Bay, and reached by way of Hanama'ulu Road east from the intersection of the Kuhio Highway (56), roughly one third of a mile, then eastward on Hehi Road, another half mile, directly to the beach. The Hanama'ulu Beach, bordered by ironwoods, and quite popular with residents and visitors alike, has a good, safe swimming area, especially suited to children, as well as picnicking, fishing and camping possibilities.

There remains yet another place of interest, Kilohana, located on the Kaumuali'i Highway (50), a little over a mile to the west of Lihue, and much to be recommended to first-time visitors to the area. Kilohana is in fact the former plantation estate of Gaylord Wilcox — head of the Grove Farm Plantation in the 1930s and 1940s — set on 35 acres, amid sugarcane fields. The estate, largely restored — partly in the Art Deco style — now houses an interesting collection of shops and art galleries, the latter displaying works of prominent Hawaiian artists, and a delightful courtyard restaurant, Gaylord's. There are also carriages here, drawn by Clydesdales, offering tours of the grounds as well as the nearby sugarcane fields.

A little to the west of Kilohana, too, on the *mauka* — inland — side of the highway (50), directly in front of the Kauai Community College, you can search out a Hawaiian Visitors Bureau marker, depicting a Hawaiian warrior, and directing visitors' gazes to a natural rock formation on the slopes of the Hoary Head Mountains, known as Queen Victoria's Profile, with a likeness, many will tell you, to the famous British monarch.

Wailua Falls

A worthwhile detour from Lihue is the Wailua Falls, which, although situated on the east side of Kauai, upriver from Wailua, are nevertheless accessed from Lihue, northwestward on Ma'alo Road (583) — which goes off Kuhio Highway (56) — some 4 miles. The Wailua Falls are one of Kauai's premier visitor attractions, and the most photographed waterfalls on the island. The falls, in fact, comprise twin waterfalls, and are indeed quite picturesque, located on the Wailua River, cascading some 80 feet, and featured in the opening scenes of TV's *Fantasy Island*. Interestingly, in the early years, the Wailua Falls were also the site of ceremonious leaps, performed by the island's chiefs to prove their courage.

In any event, the waterfalls are reached by way of a short hike from the main road, Ma'alo Road, descending, a half mile or so, to a large, natural pool at the foot of the falls. There are also some good picnicking possibilities here.

SOUTH SHORE

The South Shore of Kauai comprises, primarily, Poipu, the island's most famous beach area, and the small towns of Koloa, Lawai and Kalaheo, as well as a series of beach parks, all dotted along the southern end of the island — one of the driest and sunniest parts of Kauai.

Koloa

A good way to explore the south shore of Kauai, we might suggest, is to go first to Koloa, reached by way of Kaumuali'i Highway (50), some 6 or 7 miles west from Lihue, to the Koloa Gap — a natural pass between the Hoary Head Mountains to the south and the Waiale'ale range on the north — then Maluhia Road (520) south, another 3 miles or so, directly to Koloa. On Maluhia Road, of course, just south of the intersection of the Kaumuali'i Highway, is the Tree Tunnel, one of Kauai's most memorable landmarks, where age-old swamp mahogany trees — a species of eucalyptus from Australia — line the road on either side, along a mile-long stretch, joining overhead to form a leafy tunnel. The eucalyptus trees, interestingly, were originally planted here in 1911 — donated by plantation owner Walter Duncan McBryde — to stabilize and reclaim swampland, with the trees' root systems soaking up the excess water.

KOLOA

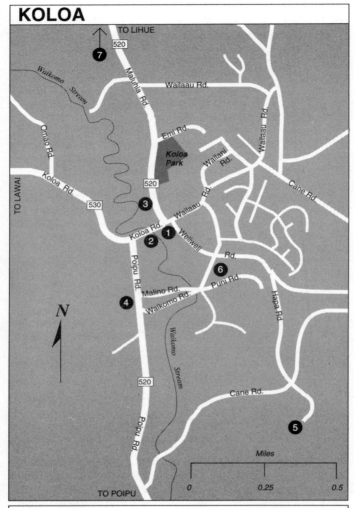

1. Old Koloa Town
2. Koloa History Center
   (Koloa Hotel)
3. Hawaii's First
   Sugar Mill
4. Koloa Church
5. St. Raphael's Church
6. Koloa Jodo Mission
7. Tree Tunnel

In any event, Koloa, meaning "long cane," is notable, first and foremost, as the birthplace of Hawaii's sugar industry, where William Hooper, of Ladd & Company of Honolulu, arrived in 1835 and established a sugar plantation — the first in the islands. A monument located near the intersection of Maluhia and Koloa roads commemorates the event and honors the industry pioneers — the first plantation owners and field workers, the latter group comprising, typically, Hawaiians, Chinese, Japanese, Portuguese, Koreans, Filipinos and Puerto Ricans. Adjacent to the monument, you can still see the remnants of the old stone chimney from the first sugar mill in Hawaii, and also view a sampling of the different sugarcane varieties found in the islands, and learn to distinguish between the various strains of the cane.

Koloa itself is a small, quaint town, tourist oriented, and with an interesting little collection of shops, boutiques, art galleries and restaurants, most of them housed in old plantation-era buildings, in a section of town, largely restored in 1984, known as Old Koloa Town. Here, too, housed in the historic, single-story Koloa Hotel, is the Koloa History Center, with several good exhibits and artifacts depicting the island's early-day sugar plantation era. The Koloa Hotel building, by the way, dates from 1898 and is situated on the banks of the Waikomo Stream.

Nearby, too, just to the south on Poipu Road, is the picturesque, New England-style Koloa Church, originally established in 1835, by Reverend Peter Gurlick, the first missionary assigned to Koloa; and to the southeast of there, at the bottom end of Hapa Road — which goes off Weliweli Road, which, in turn, goes off Koloa Road — stands the historic St. Raphael's Church, the oldest Catholic church on Kauai, originally founded in 1841, and rebuilt in 1856, from coral and lava rock.

Also of interest here, are two Japanese temples, Koloa Jodo Mission and Koloa Hongwanji, located at 3480 Waikomo Road and 5525 Koloa Road, respectively, and both dating from 1910. The temples were originally built to serve the ethnic Japanese community during the early plantation days.

Poipu

South of Koloa, of course, some 2 miles or so on Poipu Road, lies Poipu, the island's most famous beach resort, centered around the popular Poipu Beach, crescent-shaped, sandy, and sun-drenched, and quite possibly among the best beaches in Hawaii, with excellent swimming, snorkeling, surfing and boogey-boarding possibilities. There are, besides, other beaches here as well — Waiohai, Sheraton, Shipwreck, Baby Beach and Brennecke's — and a myriad of hotels and condominiums,

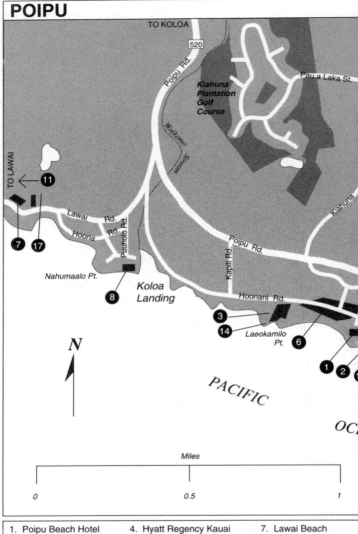

POIPU

TO KOLOA

520

Poipu Rd.

Kiahuna
Plantation
Golf
Course

Pau a Laka St.

Waikomo Stream

Kiahuna

TO LAWAI

⑪

Lawai   Rd.

Hoona   Rd.

Puuholo Rd.

⑦

⑰

Poipu Rd.

Kapili Rd.

Nahumaalo Pt.

Koloa
Landing

⑧

Hoonani Rd.

③

⑭

Laeokamilo
Pt.

⑥

①

②

①

N

PACIFIC

OC

OCE

Miles

0   0.5   1

1. Poipu Beach Hotel	4. Hyatt Regency Kauai	7. Lawai Beach Resort
2. Waiohai Beach Resort	5. Poipu Kai Resort	8. Whaler's Cove Condominiums
3. Sheraton Kauai	6. Kiahuna Plantation Condominiums	

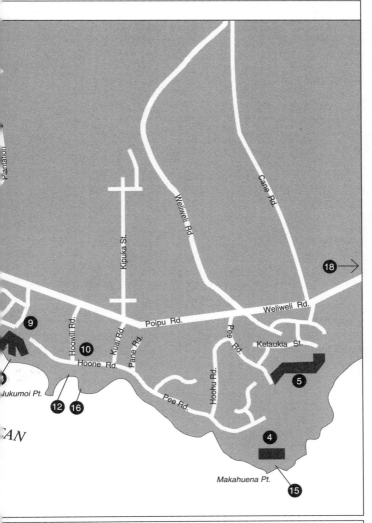

9. Moir Gardens
10. Kilahuna Heiau
11. Spouting Horn
12. Poipu Beach Park
13. Waiohai Beach
14. Sheraton Beach
15. Shipwreck Beach
16. Brennecke's Beach
17. Prince Kuhio Birthplace Monument
18. Mahaulepu

interspersed with several good restaurants and shops, and — a rarity on the island — even a shopping center.

In any event, at the west end of the Poipu Beach area — reached on Kapili Road, which goes off Poipu Road — stands the Sheraton Kauai, one of the first resort hotels developed at Poipu, in the late 1960s, situated on a 20-acre site and bordering an especially lovely, palm-fringed beach — popularly known as the Sheraton Beach — with good sunbathing, swimming, surfing and windsurfing possibilities. The hotel itself features 456 oceanview rooms, in two separate wings, 2 stories and 4 stories high, respectively, as well as three restaurants, two swimming pools, children's wading pools, and tennis courts.

Close at hand also, a quarter mile or so east of the Sheraton Kauai, on Poipu Road — on the *makai* (ocean) side of the road — is the Kiahuna Plantation Condominiums complex, fronting on the sunny Poipu Beach and situated on the former estate of Hector and Alexandra Moir, amid landscaped gardens with tropical trees and plants, and with footpaths, crossing over tiny Oriental bridges, leading down to the beach. Here, too, on the grounds of the Kiahuna Plantation are the Moir Gardens, with a delightful collection of plumeria, aloe, Hawaiian orchids, cacti, and some 4,000 varieties of plants, featured in the book, *Great Gardens of America*. Overlooking the gardens, and also of interest, is the Plantation Gardens Restaurant, housed in the former home of Mr. and Mrs. Moir, dating from 1930.

Two other hotels at Poipu, seriously damaged during the 1992 hurricane Iniki, are the 3-story Piopu Beach Hotel and the adjacent, 4-story Waiohai Resort Hotel, the latter built on the site of the old Waiohai Hotel — the first hotel at Poipu, originally built in the early 1960s. Both the Poipu Beach and Waiohai hotels are situated along Waiohai Beach, a crescent-shaped, sandy beach, with some of the best snorkeling and swimming on the island. Closeby, too, of interest to the visitor, are the ruins of a 17th-century *heiau*, the Kilahuna Heiau, located directly across from the Waiohai hotel, near a grove of palms. The Kilahuna Heiau, by the way, was one of Kauai's most important *heiaus*.

Yet another Poipu resort, farther east on Poipu Road, is the 600-room Hyatt Regency, a luxury hotel, no less, built in 1991, at a cost of $220 million, amid a great deal of controversy over the hotel's selection of its building site — believed to be an ancient Hawaiian burial ground. The hotel, however, has in it some good restaurants, swimming pools, tennis courts, and an 18-hole, Robert Trent Jones-designed golf course, sprawled over some 200 acres. The hotel itself borders on Shipwreck Beach, a partly-sandy, partly-coral-lined beach, which, nevertheless, offers excellent bodysurfing possibilities, although swimming is not encouraged, due to the strong ocean currents

The twin Wailua Falls, plunging more than 80 feet into the Wailua River

Kauai's famous Na Pali Coast

and sharp coral, making it rather unsafe for the sport.

Also of interest at Poipu, a little way to the east of the Waiohai Resort Hotel, at the foot of Hoowili Road, which goes off Poipu Road, is the Poipu Beach Park, one of the south shore's most popular beach parks. Here you can visit the Baby Beach, an especially good place for children to splash around, with a protective reef just off shore; and just to the east of there, another quarter mile or so, lies Brennecke's Beach, a small pocket of sand, but with excellent bodysurfing possibilities. The Poipu Beach Park, incidentally, also has good public facilities, including pavilions, picnic tables, and showers and restrooms.

Koloa Landing and Spouting Horn

Just west of Poipu on Hoonani Road — which can also be accessed by way of Poipu Road south, Lawai Road southwest a little way, and so to Hoonani Road — lies the historic Koloa Landing, an important port and center of commerce during the 1800s, when Koloa, the township, farther to the north, was at the heart of Hawaii's sugar industry. Koloa Landing, in fact, located at the mouth of the Waikomo Stream, was once one of the largest ports in Hawaii, used by Koloa Plantation to ship much of the island's sugar. It was also, we might add, an important whaling port in the 19th century, second only to Lahaina and Honolulu; and, for a brief period, it even served as a port of entry, with a customs officer stationed here. In the early 1900s, however, with the ascendancy of nearby Port Allen and, later on, Nawiliwili as Kauai's chief ports, Koloa Landing, for the most part, was abandoned. The landing is now used primarily by scuba divers as a staging point.

Westward from Koloa Landing on Lawai Road, a mile or so, and also with some visitor interest, is the Prince Kuhio Park, dedicated to Prince Jonah Kuhio Kalanianaloe, and where a monument marks the birthplace of the Hawaiian prince. Prince Kuhio, in fact, was born in 1871, of royal parentage, and is well remembered as Hawaii's delegate to the United States Congress, where he served from 1903 until 1922, and accomplished a great deal for the Hawaiian people — even though Hawaii, as a territory of the United States at the time, rather than a state, officially had no vote — including establishing the Hawaiian Homes Commission Act, whereby public lands have been made available to native Hawaiians for homesteading.

Close at hand, too, just west of the Prince Kuhio Park, is the Beach House Beach, a narrow, roadside beach. The beach has good sunbathing, snorkeling, surfing and bodysurfing possibilities, with three surf breaks — "PK's," "Centers," and "Acid Drop" — all with consistently good waves, especially in the summer months.

Finally, another one and one-half miles westward from the Beach House Restaurant on Lawai Road, and we are at the Spouting Horn Beach Park, which has in it, as its chief attraction, Spouting Horn, one of Hawaii's most visited blowholes. Spouting Horn is indeed quite spectacular — a natural lava tube, through which, with the pressure from the sea swells, steaming water gushes forth in a fountain, at regular intervals. But before the water, comes a loud, roaring sound from the blowhole, of rushing air and water — but which, locals will tell you, are the moans of a legendary Hawaiian *mo'o* — or lizard. The *mo'o*, we are told, was once returning from Ni'ihau to Kauai, after discovering his two sisters dead on the island of Ni'ihau; and, in his sadness, blinded by his tears, he missed the landing and, instead, became trapped in the lava tube, where you can still hear him today, moaning.

Mahaulepu

Another place of interest, while in the Koloa-Poipu area, is Mahaulepu, lying just to the east of Koloa — or northeast of Poipu — and reached by way of Poipu Road, northeastward, passing by the Hyatt Regency, to the end, then right — southeast — onto a cane road that eventually leads to the coast.

Mahaulepu, however, once a densely populated area and now largely undeveloped, filled with sugarcane fields owned by the Grove Farm Company, encompasses a 2-mile stretch of coastline, made up of three separate sections — Gillin's Beach, Kawailoa Bay and Haula Beach. The first of these, Gillin's Beach, can be reached by following the road leading to Mahaulepu to the right — southwestward — at the three-way intersection at the very bottom. Gillin's Beach itself, named for a local manager of a plantation, is a narrow, sandy beach, quite popular with surfers and windsurfers. A short walk north from Gillin's Beach, too, crossing over a stream and following it inland, leads to a series of caves, well worth exploring.

Northeast at the three-way intersection at the bottom of the road leading to Mahaulepu, a half mile or so, lies Kawailoa Bay, a lovely, unspoiled coastal area, backed by shallow sand dunes and groves of ironwood, and with magnificent sea cliffs overhanging the bay at the eastern end and a sea stack rising from the ocean just off shore. Kawailoa Bay is frequented primarily by sunbathers, swimmers and fishermen, although — a word of caution — the ocean currents along this coastal stretch can often be quite dangerous.

Beyond Kawailoa Bay, the road finally ends. However, a little walk northeast along the shoreline, will bring you to Haula

Beach, a surprisingly secluded, picturesque beach, backed by the 100-foot-high Aweoweo Sand Dunes. Haula Beach, however, offers only fair swimming conditions, due, primarily, to the coral and strong ocean currents.

Lawai and Kalaheo

Lawai is a small, rural town, which once was at the center of Kauai's pineapple industry, surrounded by fields of pineapple, and which now produces a variety of tropical fruit. The town lies approximately 10 miles west of Lihue on Kaumuali'i Highway (50), or 2 miles northwest of Koloa, reached, from the latter, more or less directly on Koloa Road.

Lawai has two places of interest for the visitor — the 186-acre National Tropical Botanical Garden, and the adjacent, 100-acre Allerton Gardens, located at the southern end of Hailima Road, which goes off Koloa Road, southward. The National Tropical Botanical Garden, one of the great botanical gems of Kauai, and the only nationally supported tropical garden, chartered by the United States Congress in 1964 and subsequently opened to public viewing in 1971, has lavish displays of plants from tropical regions throughout the world, and is notable, too, as one of the world's big tropical research gardens, especially interesting to students of botany and serious gardeners; and the nearby Allerton Gardens, originally established in 1938 by Robert Allerton and his adopted son, John Gregg Allerton, feature, among other tropical plants, several rare South Pacific plants, introduced to the island by the Allertons. At the gardens, by the way, you can also visit the site of the home of Queen Emma, wife of King Kamehameha IV, which stood here, in its original state, until 1992, when it was completely destroyed by the Hurricane Iniki. At any rate, the gardens, both the Allerton Gardens and the National Tropical Botanical Garden, can be toured by calling ahead for reservations, at (808) 332-7361.

Westward still, another 2 miles from Lawai — or 12 miles from Lihue — on the Kaumuali'i Highway lies Kalaheo — meaning "proud day" — another small town, and the westernmost on the island's south shore. Kalaheo's chief interest lies in its Kukuiolono Park, located a mile or so south from the Kaumuali'i Highway (50) on Papalina Road, at the intersection of Pu'u Road. The Kukuiolono Park has in it groves of eucalyptus, a delightful Japanese garden — quite popular for weddings, and ideal for strolling around — and a small area devoted to Hawaiian exhibits, where you can view, quite typically, such artifacts as a stone bowl, a stone salt pan, and a stone lamp, among others. There is also a 9-hole public golf course at the park, with a clubhouse, overlooking the ocean.

Also of interest at Kalaheo are the Olu Pua Gardens, roughly
a third of a mile west of mile marker 12, on the *mauka* — inland
— side of the Kaukualii Highway (50), reached by following a
sign-posted dirt road inland from the highway, a half mile or so,
to the gardens. The Olu Pua Gardens, interestingly, are situated
on the former estate of the manager of the Kauai Pineapple
Plantation, comprising some 12 acres, covered with lush gardens, featuring more than 5,000 species of tropical plants, trees
and flowers. At Olu Pua, you can also take a one-hour guided
tour of the gardens, educational, of course, and especially interesting to students of Hawaiian flora.

WEST SIDE

The West Side of Kauai — a term, no doubt, you are likely
to hear in these parts — describes, broadly, the west shore of the
island, wild and remote, including in it the towns of Hanapepe,
the most important, and Waimea and Kekaha, and also taking in,
for the purposes of touring, the famous Waimea Canyon and
Kokee State Park, lying farther inland from the coast.

Hanapepe

The major town on the west side of the island, reached on
Kaumuali'i Highway (50), is Hanapepe, some 4 miles from
Kalaheo — or 16 miles from Lihue — westward. But first,
before Hanapepe, alongside the highway, some 2 miles west of
Kalaheo, is the Hanapepe Valley Lookout, with commanding
views of the lush Hanapepe Valley, as it heads toward the center
of the island; and two miles farther, southwestward from the
lookout on the highway, lies the little town of Ele'ele, which has
in it a handful of shops and, more importantly, Port Allen, a small
boat harbor, reached on Waialo Road (Highway 541) — which
goes off Kaumuali'i Highway, south — and which, during the
late 1800s and early 1900s, before the development of Nawiliwili Harbor at Lihue in the 1930s, was Kauai's principal port.

In any event, Hanapepe is "Kauai's Biggest Little Town,"
and, indeed, the west side's largest and most important community, situated at the heart of an agriculturally rich region, which
supplies the island with much of its produce. It is also, we might
add, notable as the "Bougainvillea Capital of Hawaii", abundant
in the colorful flowers, and with hills covered with bougainvil-
leas rolling back from the highway, on the approaches to Hanapepe. The town itself, lying at the head of Hanapepe Bay, is

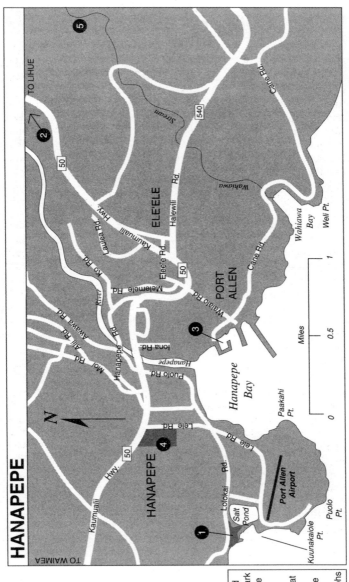

HANAPEPE

1. Salt Pond Beach Park
2. Hanapepe Valley Lookout
3. Small Boat Harbor
4. Hanapepe Park
5. Petroglyphs

filled with shops, restaurants and art galleries, and is recogniz-
able, too, from its main street, Hanapepe Road, which provided
the setting for the television mini-series, *The Thorn Birds*.

Just to the south of Hanapepe, and also of interest — reached
by way of Lele Road south off the highway (50), just past mile
marker 17, then right onto Lokokai Road, to the very end — lies
the Salt Pond Beach Park, where, on the *makai* — ocean — side
of Lokokai Road, you can see some ancient salt ponds, used by
Hawaiians, for hundreds of years, to make salt. Typically, sea
water is pumped into the ponds and left to evaporate in the sun,
leaving only the crystallized salt in the mud-lined beds, which
is then drained further, and bagged and made ready for market.
At the Salt Pond Beach Park, there are also some pavilions,
picnic tables, and showers and restroom facilities now, and the
beach, besides, has good swimming possibilities, with a protective reef just offshore.

Westward from Hanapepe, of course, lie the small, plantation
towns of Kaumakani, Olokele and Pakala, where sugar is still
the principal industry, but which have little else to interest the
visitor, save for a surf break at Pakala, known as "Pakalas" or
"Infinities," with its exceptionally long waves, especially spectacular during the summer months. There are also good views
of Ni'ihau from here, directly across the Kaulakahi Channel,
southwestward. The beach can be reached by way of a dirt trail
that dashes off through a sugarcane field, *makai* from the highway (50), at mile marker 21, to the ocean, then east a little way,
to the beach.

Farther still, another one and one-half miles west from Pakala
— 22½ miles west of Lihue — lies the Russian Fort Elizabeth
State Park, a 17-acre park, situated largely on the east bank of
the Waimea River, and where you can still see the ruins of the
Russian fort — for which the park is named — dating from 1817.
The fort was originally built for the Russians by a German
architect, Georg Anton Scheffer, and named for Czarina Elizabeth, wife of Alexander I. In 1817, however, not long after its
construction, the fort was abandoned by the Russians, and oc-
cupied by Hawaiians, until 1864, when it was finally closed. A
self-guided walk leads past remnants of a fort wall, with its
star-like projections, where canons were once placed, and
through the fort, where you can still see the layout of the
quarters, armory and barracks.

Waimea

The next major town, northwestward on Kaumuali'i Highway, a half mile or so from the Fort Elizabeth state park, just
over the Waimea River, is Waimea, with its associations to

WAIMEA

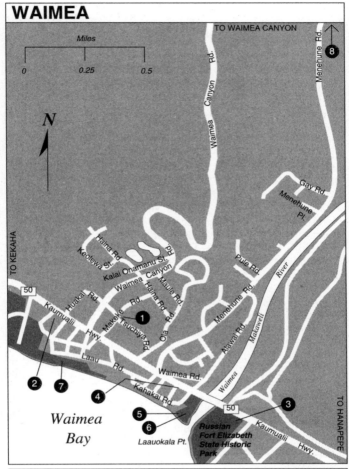

TO WAIMEA CANYON

Miles

0   0.25   0.5

N

TO KEKAHA

TO HANAPEPE

Waimea Bay

Canyon Rd.

Waimea Canyon Rd.

Menehune Rd.

Gay Rd.

Menehune Pl.

Pule Rd.

River

Haina Rd.

Keolewa St.

Kalai Onamanu St.

Waimea Canyon Rd.

Maule Rd.

Haina Rd.

Kaumualii Hwy.

Huakai Rd.

Makeke Rd.

Tsuchiya Rd.

Ola Rd.

50

Menehune Rd.

Atawai Rd.

Makaweli

Laau Rd.

Waimea Rd.

Kahakai Rd.

Waimea

50

Kaumualii Hwy.

Laauokala Pt.

Russian Fort Elizabeth State Historic Park

1. Waimea Foreign Church
2. Site of Waimea Hawaiian Church
3. Russian Fort
4. Captain Cook Statue
5. Captain Cook Landing Place
6. Lucy Wright Beach Park
7. Waimea Recreational Pier State Park
8. Menehune Ditch

Captain James Cook. Waimea, in fact, is the site of Cook's first landing in Hawaii, on January 20, 1778. A statue of Captain Cook is located in the center of town, on the highway itself, and a plaque, also commemorating his landing, is located at the Lucy Wright Beach Park — at the actual site of the landing, on the west bank of the Waimea River — which lies on the *makai* — ocean — side of the highway, as you enter the town of Waimea. The park, besides, has some public facilities — including showers and restrooms — as well as some camping possibilities and a beach with scattered driftwood.

Waimea was also the first place on the island to host western missionaries. There is, in fact, one of the island's most notable, missionary era churches located here, of interest to the visitor. The Waimea Foreign Church, a New England-style church, dating from 1859 and constructed from stone blocks, is situated at the corner of Tsuchiya Road and Makeke Road; it was, interestingly, 12 years in the making! Another church, the Waimea Hawaiian Church, originally built in 1872, stood on Kaumuali'i Highway (50), near the corner of Hale Road, until it was completely destroyed in 1992 by the hurricane Iniki. The site of the church, however, can be visited.

Another place of interest here, located just to the north of the Waimea township, some 1½ miles on the Menehune Road, which heads out from the center of town, off Kaumuali'i Highway, is the ancient Menehune Ditch — a feat of engineering, no less, attributed to Kauai's legendary — and industrious — little people, the *menehune*. The *menehune*, we are told, were a mysterious people, who worked only at night, and completed entire projects in the course of a single night. Their ingenuity, dexterity, and knowledge of construction can be seen in some of the early-day architectural examples found in the islands, attributed to them, with the flanged and fitted cut-stone bricks interlocking in a manner, unique to the *menehune*. The Menehune Ditch — or what is left of it — is perhaps the most famous work of these pixie-like, ancient people. The ditch, of course, was originally built as an aqueduct, some 24 feet high, to irrigate the *taro* patches in the valley. Today, however, only a small portion of the ditch is visible, although it remains a marvel of no small measure.

Kekaha

Kekaha, the next town along, some 3 miles west of Waimea on Kaumuali'i Highway, is essentially a sugar plantation town, which has at the center of it the Kekaha Sugar Mill, and where the principal industry is, yes, sugar.

Kekaha, however, also has in it the Kekaha Beach Park,

situated near the northwest end of town, and which, most importantly, marks the beginning of a pristine white-sand beach, secluded, even desolate, stretching some 12 miles along the largely uninhabited western corner of the island, to the Polihale State Park, farther to the north. Kekaha Beach, however, is frequented primarily by surfers and fishermen, with swimming not advisable here, due to the strong rip currents and longshore currents in the ocean.

Approximately midway between the Kekaha Beach Park and Polihale State Park, off the highway (50), is the Pacific Missile Range Facility, an area used for underwater missile testing and rocket launches, owned and operated by the U.S. Navy. Here, too, is Majors Bay, a popular beach, and one of the best places on the west side for surfing, accessed through the naval base. And again, swimming is not encouraged here, due to the unsafe ocean conditions.

Finally, at Polihale State Park, the road ends. Polihale — also known as "Barking Sands," due to the crunching sound the sand makes underfoot — is one of the most beautiful beaches in the Hawaiian islands, some 4 miles long and almost a hundred yards wide, on the average, backed by sand dunes, 50-100 feet high, and overhung, at its northern end, by lofty sea cliffs, situated at the beginning — or southwestern end — of the fabulous Na Pali Coast. The Polihale State Park, however, is reached by way of Kaumuali'i Highway, a mile or so past the Pacific Missile Range Facility, then left — toward the coast — on a sign-posted, bumpy dirt road, another 3½ miles, passing through fields of sugarcane, to a large monkey pod tree, situated at a fork in the road; at the fork, go right — or north — a little over one and one-half miles, directly to the Polihale State Park day use area, where there are some pavilions with picnic tables, and showers and restrooms facilities. Once again, be forewarned, the ocean conditions here are unsafe for swimming, with strong, unpredictable currents.

Also in the Polihale area, of interest to visitors, is a coastal strip known as Queen's Pond, named for a Kauaian queen who once bathed here, and reached on the same Polihale dirt road — which goes off the highway (50) — to the monkey pod tree at the fork, then left — or south — a little way to Queen's Pond. There is, surprisingly, a safe swimming area here, protected by a reef just offshore, although high surf waves are known to frequently crash over the reef, creating unusually strong currents, especially during the winter months.

Waimea Canyon

There are two routes leading into the Waimea Canyon, located in the western part of the island, more or less directly north
of Waimea. The first of these, Kokee Road, heads out from
Kekaha, northeastward, with views of the ocean and Kekaha
township; and the other, quite possibly the more popular of the
two, and more scenic, the Waimea Canyon Drive, goes directly
north from Waimea, some 6 miles *mauka* — inland — to inter-
sect Kokee Road, then onward, through Waimea Canyon, to
finally emerge at the Kokee State Park. Along the Waimea route,
too, some 4 miles from the intersection of Kaumuali'i Highway,
is a roadside lookout, at an elevation of 1,000 feet, with sweeping views of the canyon, and, to the south, of the town of Waimea
and the Pacific Ocean beyond. Also worth stopping at, is the
Kukui Trailhead, at an elevation of 3,000 feet, from where the
Iliau Nature Trail takes you around a half-mile loop, offering
panoramic views of the canyon, and from where, also, the Kukui
Trail leads along a strenuous, 2½-mile hike, descending some
2,500 feet to the Waimea River.

In any event, Waimea Canyon is famous as the "Grand Canyon
of the Pacific" — a 2,850-foot-deep canyon, 10 miles long and 2
miles wide, carved, over time, by rivers and streams and the
weather, and quite spectacular with its maze of gullies and spires,
in deep hues of red, brown and green, continually changing in the
light. There are, by the way, three notable lookouts here — the
Waimea Canyon Lookout, Pu'u ka Pele Overlook, and the Pu'u
Hinahina Viewpoint — all offering different perspectives on the
canyon. The Waimea Canyon Lookout, of course, is at an elevation
of 3,400 feet, and offers superb views of the canyon walls and
various streams emerging from the center of the island, at
Wai'ale'ale. Some 3 miles farther, at the Pu'u ka Pele Overlook,
you can see the Waipoo Falls, cascading some 800 feet — that is,
if there has been some rain — and another mile from there is the
Pu'u Hinahina Viewpoint, where there are two lookouts, one with
views of the island and the town of Hanapepe, and the other
overlooking the nearby island of Ni'ihau.

Kokee State Park

Northward from Waimea Canyon lies the Kokee State Park,
at an elevation of 3,600 feet, encompassing more than 4,600
acres, and with several miles of hiking trails, scores of picturesque waterfalls, and scenic vistas throughout. The temperatures
at Kokee, typically, are 10°-15° lower than at sea level; and here,

WAIMEA CANYON

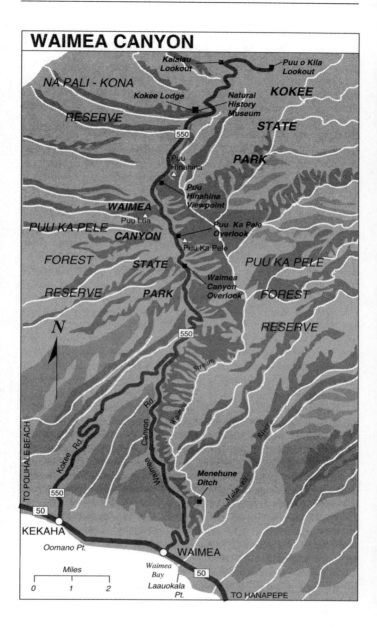

Kalalau Lookout

Puu o Kila Lookout

NA PALI - KONA

Kokee Lodge

Natural History Museum

KOKEE

RESERVE

STATE

550

PARK

Puu Hinahina

Puu Hinahina Viewpoint

WAIMEA

Puu Lua

PUU KA PELE

Puu Ka Pele Overlook

CANYON

Puu Ka Pele

FOREST

STATE

PUU KA PELE

Waimea Canyon Overlook

RESERVE

PARK

FOREST

RESERVE

N

550

Waimea Stream

Waimea River

Kokee Rd.

Waimea Canyon Rd.

Makaweli River

Menehune Ditch

TO POLIHALE BEACH

550

50

KEKAHA

Oomano Pt.

Miles

0   1   2

WAIMEA

Waimea Bay

50

Laauokala Pt.

TO HANAPEPE

too, on Kokee Road, some 2 miles north of the Pu'u Hinahina Viewpoint, are the Kokee Lodge — with rental cabins, and serving breakfast, lunch and dinner — and the adjacent Natural History Museum, which has a good display of Hawaiian artifacts and information on the area's wildlife, and an excellent book section concentrating on Hawaiiana, where you can also find maps — including trail maps — for the area. Additionally, at the museum you can obtain current information on the area's trails, including an update on trail conditions.

Indeed, among the most popular pursuits at the Kokee State Park, as many will attest, is hiking, with a variety of trails — for all levels of fitness and training — and well-marked trailheads throughout the park. Here, for instance, on Kokee Road itself, on either side of mile marker 17, are the Awa'awa'puhi and Kalua'puhi trailheads, with trails leading down into the valley, and 2 miles farther, more or less at the end of Kokee Road, are trailheads for trails leading into the Alakai Swamp, which lies just below Mount Wai'ale'ale — the latter at an elevation of 5,148 feet and notable as the wettest spot on earth — and which is responsible for feeding many of the streams on Kauai, filtering much of the rain water here — an average of 451 inches each year! — into the scores of streams and rivers. Hiking through the Alakai Swamp can be challenging, but rewarding, with trails leading through native rain forests and bogs, where you might, indeed, find yourself knee-deep in mud.

Also at the Kokee State Park are the Kalalau Lookout and the Pu'u o Kila Lookout, located at mile marker 18 and at the end of Kokee Road, respectively, and both with good views of the Kalalau Valley, where an ancient Hawaiian settlement once flourished, with little or no contact with the outside world, until the growing urban centers of the island lured the last of the inhabitants from this lush valley. The Kalalau Lookout, by the way, at an elevation of 4,000 feet, also overlooks the astonishing Na Pali Coast to the north.

EAST SIDE

The East Side of Kauai, more populous — and more fertile — than the west side or even the south shore of the island, takes in the area extending from just north of Lihue to Moloa'a Bay at the northeastern corner of the island, including in it the towns of Wailua and Kapa'a, the most important, as well as the tourist-alluring Fern Grotto and one of Hawaii's largest coconut groves.

Wailua

The first place of note on the east side of Kauai is Wailua, one of the oldest towns on this part of the island, situated some 6 miles north of Lihue on Kuhio Highway (56), at the mouth of the Wailua River — Hawaii's only navigable river, the source of which is Mount Wai'ale'ale (elevation, 5,148 feet) at the center of the island, notable as the wettest spot on earth, with an average annual rainfall of 451 inches. The low-lying coastal area surrounding the Wailua River, by the way, where the river drains into the ocean, was once one of the most sacred places in Hawaii, dotted with scores of *heiaus* and places of refuge — there are seven sacred *heiaus* still there — from where the *ali'i* — or chiefs — would make their pilgrimage, along the river, to the altar at the top of Wai'ale'ale. The lower end of the Wailua River, however, now part of the Wailua River State Park, is a popular recreation area, ideally suited to waterskiing, kayaking, and even fishing. The Wailua River State Park, incidentally, takes in the Wailua Beach Park, Lydgate State Park, parts of the Wailua River bank, Fern Grotto, and most of the *heiaus* in the area.

At Lydgate State Park, — located on the coast just to the south of the mouth of the Wailua River, and reached on Kuhio Highway (56) north from Lihue some 5 miles, then off on Leho Drive, a half mile, to Nalu Road, which leads directly to the park — there are good swimming, picnicking, fishing and beach-combing possibilities, making it especially attractive for family recreation. The beach at the park, in fact, offers some of the safest swimming conditions on the island, with a boulder break-water built to protect it from the shorebreak here. Also, a little way north along the beach at Lydgate Park, you can visit the site of the Hauola Place of Refuge, marked by a plaque, where breakers of *kapu* would go to atone for their sins, before being permitted back into society.

Just south of the Wailua River, too, on the *mauka* — inland — side of Kuhio Highway (56), is the Wailua Marina, from where cruise boats depart daily, up the Wailua River, for the much-publicized Fern Grotto — an amphitheater-like cave, with huge, overhanging ferns inside it, and which also produces some extraordinarily wonderful acoustics. Fern Grotto is also the setting for hundreds of weddings every year, and the boat trips, typically, feature live Hawaiian music, including in their score the Hawaiian Wedding Song and other Hawaiian melodies.

Also at the Wailua Marina is Smith's Tropical Paradise, a 30-acre cultural and botanical garden, where self-guided tours lead along paths criss-crossing the gardens, past a variety of Kauai's exotic plants, flowers and trees. There are also Japanese, Filipino and Polynesian villages built on the grounds here,

WAILUA

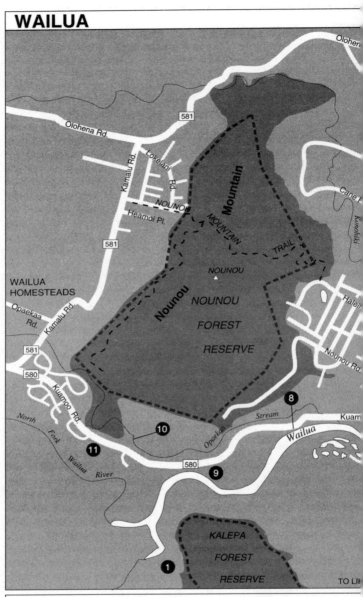

1. Fern Grotto
2. Wailua Beach
3. Smith's Tropical Paradise
4. Hauola Place of Refuge
5. Holoholoku Heiau
6. Keahua Arboretum
7. Royal Birthstones
8. Bellstone
9. Poliahu Heiau
10. Opaekaa Falls
11. Kamokila Hawaiian Village
12. Coconut Plantation Market Place
13. Royal Coconut Grove

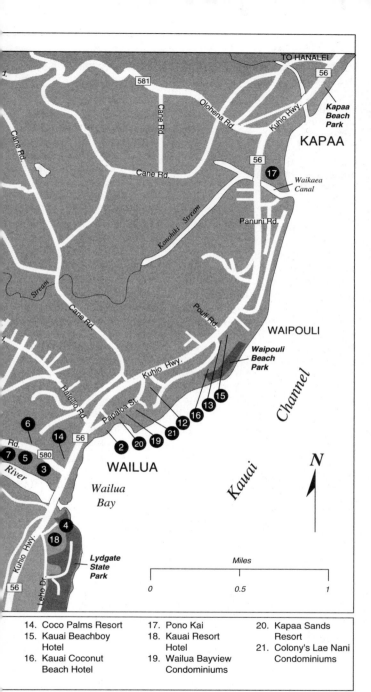

14. Coco Palms Resort	17. Pono Kai	20. Kapaa Sands Resort
15. Kauai Beachboy Hotel	18. Kauai Resort Hotel	21. Colony's Lae Nani Condominiums
16. Kauai Coconut Beach Hotel	19. Wailua Bayview Condominiums	

celebrating the cultural and ethnic mix of the people of Kauai; and each night, a garden luau and international show showcases the foods and entertainment of Tahiti, Hawaii, China, Japan, the Philippines, New Zealand and Samoa.

North of the mouth of the Wailua River, of course, lies the Wailua Beach Park, a half-mile-long beach, extending from the river mouth north to a rocky point on the coast, alongside the highway (56). Wailua Beach is a popular beach, although swimming is not encouraged, due to the strong rip tides at various points along the coast here, especially near the mouth of the river.

On the *mauka* — inland — side of the Wailua Beach Park, stands the famous Coco Palms Hotel, a 45-acre resort, originally built in 1953, on the site of an ancient royal court, and featuring thatched roof cottages with Polynesian decor, lagoons, and one of the largest coconut groves in Hawaii, with over 2,000 coconut palms. Coco Palms, in fact, epitomizes Hawaiiana, and, over the years, has provided the setting for such Hollywood hits as *South Pacific*, *Blue Hawaii*, starring Elvis Presley, and *Sadie Thompson*, starring Rita Hayworth, for which a wedding chapel was built here. Visitors, not unlike the hotel's guests, can tour the Coco Palms grounds at leisure, and are also invited to watch the torch-lighting ceremony each night, which begins at dusk.

Two other resorts of interest in the area, the Outrigger Kauai Beach Hotel and Kauai Coconut Beach Hotel, are located just to the south and northeast of the Coco Palms Resort, on Kuhio Highway. The first of these, the Outrigger Kauai Beach Hotel, comprising a series of low-rise 4-story buildings, boasts 350 guest rooms, 3 swimming pools — with the main pool area landscaped with caves — and fountains and waterfalls; and the other, the Kauai Coconut Beach Hotel, is set amid 11 acres of towering coconut palms along Waipouli Beach, and has 309 well-appointed rooms in a multi-winged building. There are, besides, other notable resort hotels here, including the Aston Kauai and the 243-room Kauai Beachboy Hotel, the latter also situated among coconut palms, along a 1-mile stretch of Waipouli Beach.

West from Wailua and the Coco Palms Resort, a worthwhile detour leads along Highway 580, directly inland, journeying alongside the Wailua River, past a handful of archaeological sites, to the Opaeka'a Falls and, farther, to the Keahua Arboretum. At the very outset, however, roughly three quarters of a mile from the Kuhio Highway intersection, are the Poaiahu Arboretum, featuring a small stand of trees, located alongside the highway; and, directly across the highway from there, the ancient Holoholoku Heiau, a temple of human sacrifices, for those unfortunate enough to fail to escape to the nearby Hauola Place of Refuge.

Poipu Beach, Poipu

Golfing at the Prince Course in Princeville

Near to the arboretum and Holoholoku Heiau also, are the Royal Birthstones, Pohaku Ho'o Hanau, where, we are told, mothers of royal lineage would come to give birth to their babies — future kings and queens, no less. Following the birth of the child, the child's umbilical cord would be wedged into a crack in another sacred stone here, Pohaku Piko, to foretell the child's future: typically, if the cord was eaten up by a rat, the child, sadly, would become a thief; if not, glory to the child, for he would become a prosperous *ali'i* — or chief. Also, in accordance with a long-standing custom, the newborn *ali'i* would be carried by *kahunas* (Hawaiian priests) — such that the baby's feet not touch the ground — up the river to a bellstone, which, when struck in the appropriate manner, would resound throughout the valley, alerting all the inhabitants of the area to the arrival of the newborn *ali'i*. The bellstone, of course, is located just east of the Poliahu Heiau, off Highway 580, at the end of a dirt road, from where you can also enjoy good, commanding views of the Wailua River and the Pacific Ocean beyond.

Close at hand, too, located on the south side of the highway, just before reaching the Opaekaa Falls, is the Poliahu Heiau, a personal temple of the ruling chiefs, built, we are told, by Kauai's mysterious little people, the *menehune*. The *heiau*, named for the Hawaiian goddess of snow, Poliahu, is situated on a hill overlooking the surrounding area, filled with valleys, and the Wailua River and Pacific Ocean.

Farther still, nearly 2 miles from the Kuhio Highway (56) turnoff, are the well-visited Opaekaa Falls, wide, and cascading some 40 feet; and just past the waterfalls, a little way, lies the Kamokila Hawaiian Village, a recreated Hawaiian village, open to public viewing. Informative guided tours lead past thatched huts and a variety of native plants and trees — including patches of *taro*, from which the Hawaiian staple, *poi*, is made — explaining to visitors the applied uses for each. The ancient crafts of weaving mats and skirts are also demonstrated here.

Finally, another 4 or 5 miles — almost 7 miles from the Kuhio Highway turnoff — is the Keahua Arboretum, which is in fact part of the U.S. Forest Preserve, a lovely, secluded area, ideal for picnicking, as well as swimming in the Keahua Stream. There are some good hiking possibilities here, including a half-mile trail that loops through groves of eucalyptus and monkey pod trees, and a scenic, 2-mile trail that journeys over the Kuilau Ridge. Also of interest, 150 yards or so from the parking area, is a natural pool, ideal for swimming, and with a rope tied to an overhanging branch of a tree, enabling you to swing out over the water.

North from Wailua

Immediately north of Wailua lies the tiny community of Waipouli, which has as its chief — perhaps only — attraction, the Coconut Plantation Marketplace, situated on the *makai* — ocean — side of the Kuhio Highway (56), about a mile from the Coco Palms hotel in Wailua. The Coconut Plantation Marketplace offers excellent shopping possibilities, with a myriad of shops and boutiques, retailing everything from the rare, expensive Ni'ihau shell leis to relatively inexpensive clothing and souvenirs. There are also some worthwhile eateries and restaurants here, as well as a theater, and on Mondays, Wednesdays, Fridays and Saturdays, a popular, free-of-charge Polynesian-style *hula* show is featured at the marketplace.

Just north from Waipouli, too, from Kipuni Place, on the west side of the highway (56), you can view the Nounou Mountain Range, also known as the "Sleeping Giant." Legend endures that the huge giant once lay asleep — in the very same place that he lies now — while the island of Kauai was being invaded; and the *menehune* tried, in vain, to awaken him, throwing rocks at him, which bounced off the giant and landed on the invading army, eventually defeating it. Some of the rocks, however, as the *menehune* later discovered, had lodged in the giant's throat, thus killing him in his sleep.

In any case, there are two separate trails leading to the summit of Nounou Mountain, climbing more than 1,000 feet, and with good, all-round views of the surrounding area. The east-side trailhead, which is approximately 2 miles from the summit, is located just off Haleilio Road, a mile west of Kuhio Highway in Wailua; and the west-side trail, which journeys some one and one-half miles to the top of the mountain, begins a quarter of a mile north of mile marker 4 on Kamalu Road (Highway 581), which goes off Kuamo'o Road (Highway 580).

Farther still, another 2 miles or so — 8 miles from Lihue — and we are at Kapa'a, a former sugar and pineapple plantation town that has emerged as Kauai's most populous city, ahead of even Lihue, with a population of over 8,000. Kapa'a, however, is filled with several restored, 19th-century storefronts and buildings, housing, quite typically, souvenir and clothing shops and other tourist-oriented businesses. Here, too, on Niu Road, which goes off Kuhio Highway, heading north, is the Kapa'a Beach Park, a narrow, sandy beach which attracts, primarily, fishermen, as well as some dedicated swimmers; and just to the north of there, also alongside Kuhio Highway, lie several more, quite lovely beaches.

North from Kapa'a, Kuhio Highway (56) journeys through sugarcane fields and wide-open spaces, passing by, just out from town, a lookout with spectacular views of the east coast of the island. Here, also, some 2 miles from Kapa'a, at mile marker 10, is Kealia Beach, situated alongside the highway. Kealia is of course a delightful, crescent-shaped, sandy beach, stretching approximately a half mile between two rocky points, especially popular with surfing and bodysurfing enthusiasts. Swimming, however, is inadvisable for the most part, due to the strong, unsafe ocean currents, although, during calm weather, a small jetty at the north end of the beach offers a somewhat protected area for swimming.

North from Kealia Beach, a little over one and one-half miles, lies Donkey Beach, a picturesque, crescent-shaped, windswept beach, surrounded by ironwoods, naupaka and ilima, tucked away from the highway, with a well-worn trail leading down from the highway to the beach. The beach is especially popular with nudists, although — a word of caution — nude bathing at public beaches is prohibited by law in the state of Hawaii. The beach, however, quite interestingly, is named for the mules — mistaken, in the past, for donkeys — to be seen grazing in the pasture directly behind the beach, used by the Lihue Plantation Company to carry cane seed and bags of fertilizer to the nearby fields.

Next up, another mile or so on Kuhio Highway, is Anahola, a small town bathed in fragrant plumeria, set aside, in part, for Hawaiian homesteads. The only place of visitor interest here, however, reached on Kukuihale Road — which goes off the highway at mile marker 13 — is the Anahola Beach Park, a long, thin beach, bordered by ironwoods, and which also has some picnic tables and restroom facilities. There is a safe swimming area here, protected by a reef, although, when the surf is up, dangerous under-currents can occur, making swimming in these waters inadvisable.

A little farther, just north of mile marker 15, looking toward the mountains you can see the Anahola Mountain Range, and through it, the Hole-in-the-Mountain, now almost closed by a landslide, but with a patch of daylight still showing through. Legend has it that the hole was created when a fierce warrior, when engaged in battle with another warrior, flung his spear in rage, from Koloa, piercing the mountains here, and eventually landing farther northwest in Hanalei.

At any rate, northward, approximately a half mile past mile marker 16 on Kuhio Highway, at the corner of Ko'olau Road, is the Sunrise Fruit Stand, where you can sample fresh island fruit as well as delicious fruit smoothies; and a little way from there, at the end of Moloa'a Road — which goes off Ko'olau Road, just over a mile from the fruit stand — lies Moloa'a Beach, an idyllic, crescent-shaped beach, thoroughly secluded, and a great place for beachcombing and collecting sea shells. And again, a word of caution — the prevailing rip tides and a shore break make the ocean here rather unsafe for swimming.

NORTH SHORE

The North shore of Kauai, for all practical purposes, begins near Kepuhi Point, just east of Kilauea, and takes in the lush, green northern portion of the island, across to Ke'e Beach — at the northeastern end of the Na Pali Coast — including in it, besides Kilauea, the Princeville-Hanalei area, the tiny villages of Wainiha and Haena, and Lumahai Beach, one of Hawaii's most famous beaches.

Kilauea

Kilauea, the first town reached on Kauai's north shore, is situated on the northeast corner of the island, some 15 miles from Kapa'a (or 23 miles from Lihue) on the Kuhio Highway (56). But before Kilauea, there are two beaches of interest — Waiakalua Iki Beach and Waiakalua Nui Beach, reached on North Waiakalua Road, which goes off the highway, some three quarters of a mile past mile marker 20, toward the ocean, then left at the end of Waiakalua Road, onto a dirt road, another quarter mile or so to the end, from where a short, steep trail leads down to Waiakalua Iki Beach, with Waiakalua Nui Beach adjoining to the west of it. The Waiakalua Iki and Waiakalua Nui beaches are both quite scenic, in secluded settings, and with good beachcombing possibilities. Swimming, however, is not encouraged, due to the coral and unpredictable ocean currents.

In any case, Kilauea is a former sugar plantation town, founded in the late 1870s by the Kilauea Sugar Plantation Company, which operated here for nearly a century, until 1970. The town, typically, is small, rural, and filled with plantation-era buildings — all, surprisingly, built from stone, constituting what is considered to be the most extensive use of lava rock in the islands. Among the best examples of this rock construction is of course the Christ Memorial Episcopal Church, a quaint, coral rock church, with a hand-carved altar and stained-glass windows imported from England, dating from 1941 and located on Kolo Road, which goes off Kuhio Highway, a quarter mile or so past mile marker 23. Another, the Kong Lung Company Building, also built from lava rock, in 1941, is located on Kilauea Road, heading *makai* — toward the ocean.

Besides the town itself, Kilauea has one or two other points of interest quite close to it. Here, for instance, just to the north of town on Kilauea Road, at the very end of the road, is the Kilauea Point National Wildlife Refuge, a spectacular, 160-acre coastal park that includes in it Kilauea Point — the northernmost point on Kauai and, therefore, on the main Hawaiian islands —

and the 568-foot Crater Hill and Molokea Point, lying just to the east. The wildlife refuge, however, is a nesting colony for endangered seabirds, including red-footed boobies, wedge-tailed shearwaters, laysan albatross and the great frigate birds, all of which can be seen here, along this rugged coastline, from Kilauea Point. From here, too, it is possible to see various marine life, especially during the winter and spring months, including whales, dolphins, seals and sea turtles. Also of interest here, situated on Kilauea Point, is the old Kilauea Lighthouse, originally built in 1913, and which once featured a 4-ton Fresnel Lens — a beacon for passing ships for some 67 years, until it was finally replaced in 1980 by a smaller, more powerful light. The lighthouse is now a National Historic Landmark.

There are also a handful of beaches of interest near Kilauea. The first, Kahili Beach, also known as Quarry Beach — named for the nearby quarry — can be reached by way of Kilauea Road, a quarter mile or so north of the Kong Lung Center, then off on an unmarked, four-wheel-drive-only dirt road, eastward, another one and one-half miles, to the beach. The beach, in any case, is quite popular with surfers as well as fishermen, where you can also watch the fishermen casting their out-size nets. Swimming, again, is not encouraged, except in calm seas, due to the rip tides.

Another beach, the Kauapea Beach, popularly known as Secret Beach — even though everyone knows about it — lies more or less directly to the northwest of Kilauea, reached on Kuhio Highway west from the town, a half mile or so, then Kalihiwai Road a little way to a dirt road, which heads out north to the beach parking area, from where a well-worn trail leads down to the beach. Secret Beach, however, is a long, wide, white-sand beach, picturesque and secluded, extending from Kilauea Point westward, and increasingly popular with nudists — even though nude bathing at public beaches is prohibited in the state of Hawaii. Swimming, nevertheless, as with other beaches on the north shore, is not advised, due to strong undercurrents and high surf, especially during winter and spring months.

On Kalihiwai Road, too, is Kalihiwai Beach, a wide, sandy beach, bordered by ironwood trees, and quite popular with surfers, with its shorebreak and excellent surf — which, conversely, are detrimental to swimming, making the latter unsafe in the ocean here. For kayakers, however, there is the Kalihiwai River, which winds past several sparkling waterfalls, draining into the ocean near the west end of the beach.

Westward from Kilauea also, one and one-half miles on Kuhio Highway (56), at mile marker 25, is the Kalihiwai Valley Overlook, with sweeping views of the Kalihiwai Valley, dotted with waterfalls, and Kalihiwai River below. A little way east from the overlook on the highway, too, you can view a magnificent waterfall, on the *mauka* — inland — side of the highway.

Westward still, a half mile or so, located along Anini Road — which goes off Kalihiwai Road, which, in turn, goes off Kuhio Highway, westward, roughly a half mile past mile marker 25 — is the Anini Beach Park, a surprisingly popular beach, protected by one of the longest and widest reefs in the islands, some 2 miles long, lying a quarter mile or so offshore. The beach park has picnic tables, some of them sheltered, as well as showers and restroom facilities. The beach also offers good windsurfing, snorkeling, fishing and beachcombing possibilities, and directly across from the park, on the opposite side of Anini Road, are the Polo Grounds, which host polo matches on Sundays, during the spring and summer months.

Princeville and Hanalei

Princeville, situated some 28 miles north of Lihue on Kauai's north shore, is a major resort development, with luxury hotels and condominiums and an exclusive residential community, sprawled on 11,000 acres of prime, oceanfront land, overlooking Hanalei Bay, backed by the Hanalei Valley, and the Pacific Ocean. Interestingly, in 1860, a pioneer settler, Robert C. Wyllie, acquired the Princeville acreage and attempted to establish a sugar plantation, but quickly found the climate to be too wet and cool, unsuited to the cultivation of sugarcane. In any case, Wyllie, following a visit by King Kamehameha IV and his wife, Queen Emma, together with their 2-year-old son, Prince Ka Haku o Hawaii, named the resort "Princeville," in honor of the young prince.

At Princeville, however, at the heart of the resort is the multi-million-dollar Princeville Hotel, situated on the lookout point at Hanalei Bay, Pu'u Poa Point, and built in descending tiers down the face of the cliff. The hotel, originally developed in 1985 and renovated in 1989 at a cost of $120 million, boasts 252 luxury guest rooms with views, three well-appointed restaurants, trendy shops and boutiques, an Olympic-size swimming pool, more than 20 tennis courts, and an in-house, 64-seat cinema where you can watch — what else? — reruns of South Pacific, the 1950s classic, and From Here To Eternity, among others. Near the Princeville Hotel, too, are two world-class golf courses — the famous, 27-hole Makai Course, ranked among the top 100 courses in the country by Golf Digest; and the recently-completed Prince Course, a championship, 18-hole course — both designed by Robert Trent Jones, Jr., who, by the way, maintains a home here, in nearby Hanalei.

Princeville's other major development is the Hanalei Bay Resort, with 200 luxury units, housed in 2- and 3-story buildings, overlooking historic Hanalei Bay and the ocean. The Hanalei Bay Resort also has in it a gourmet restaurant — which features traditional Hawaiian luaus on certain nights of the week — and well-stocked shops, a sand-bottom pool, a dozen or so tennis courts, and golf at the nearby Princeville Resort golf courses. There are, besides, one or two other condominium complexes here as well, with good, comfortable accommodations, and a small commuter airport, located just off the Kuhio Highway (56), on the *mauka* — inland — side of the road.

Princeville also has two beaches of interest — Sea Lodge Beach and Pu'u Poa Beach. Sea Lodge Beach, of course, comprises a small, secluded cove, reached by way of Kamehameha Road — which goes off Kahaku Road, the main road leading into Princeville from Kuhio Highway — to the very end, at the Sea Lodge Condominiums, from where a short walk leads past the condominiums — between blocks B and C, and around block A, on the ocean side — following the coastline west, and so to the beach. The second beach, Pu'u Poa Beach, one of the most popular in the Princeville area, is situated more or less at the foot of the Princeville Hotel, with a public right-of-way leading down to the beach. The Pu'u Poa Beach itself is a long, sandy beach, protected by a fringe reef, which makes this an especially good place for snorkeling, in calm seas.

In any event, west from Princeville, at mile marker 28, the Kuhio Highway (56) becomes Highway 560 — with the mileage markers beginning again, at 0 — and a little way from there, on the *mauka* — inland — side of the highway is the Hanalei Valley Lookout, overlooking, naturally, the fertile Hanalei Valley, 6 miles long and one mile wide, covered with fields of *taro*, the Hawaiian staple. Here, too, in the Hanalei Valley is the 917-acre Hanalei National Wildlife Refuge, established in 1972 as a sanctuary for indigenous water birds. Besides which, from the overlook, looking down, you can also see the Hanalei River below, crossed over by an arched, one-lane highway bridge, the Hanalei Bridge, built in 1912, which leads into Hanalei.

The town of Hanalei itself, situated approximately a mile west from Hanalei Bridge, at the head of Hanalei Bay, is a characteristic north shore town, rural, unhurried, and set in lush, green surroundings. It has in it several small shops, a handful of restaurants, one or two museums, and a church of historic interest, the Wai'oli Hui'ia Church, located just west of mile marker 3 on the *mauka* (inland) side of the highway (560). The Wai'oli Hui'ia Church was originally built in 1834 by Reverend William P. Alexander and his wife, Mary Ann — notably the first missionaries to arrive in Hanalei — and rebuilt in 1912. Also, just to the back of the church is the Wai'oli Mission House

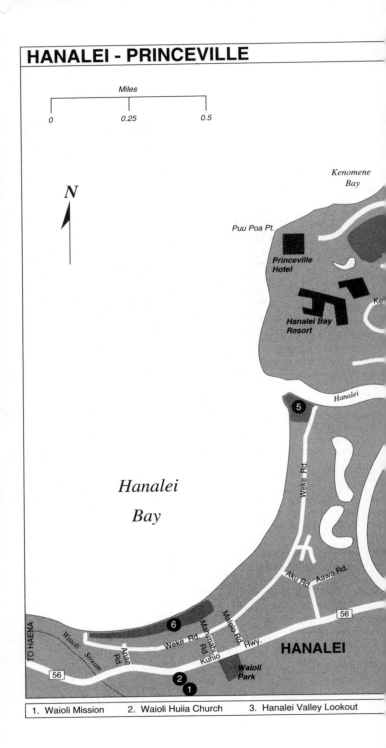

HANALEI - PRINCEVILLE

Miles

0   0.25   0.5

N

Kenomene
Bay

Puu Poa Pt.

Princeville
Hotel

Hanalei Bay
Resort

Ke

Hanalei

5

Weke Rd.

Hanalei
Bay

Aku Rd. Aawa Rd.

56

6

TO HAENA

Waioli Stream

Anae Rd.

Weke Rd.

Mahimahi Rd.

Maiolo Rd.

Kuhio Hwy.

HANALEI

Waioli
Park

56

2

1

1. Waioli Mission   2. Waioli Huiia Church   3. Hanalei Valley Lookout

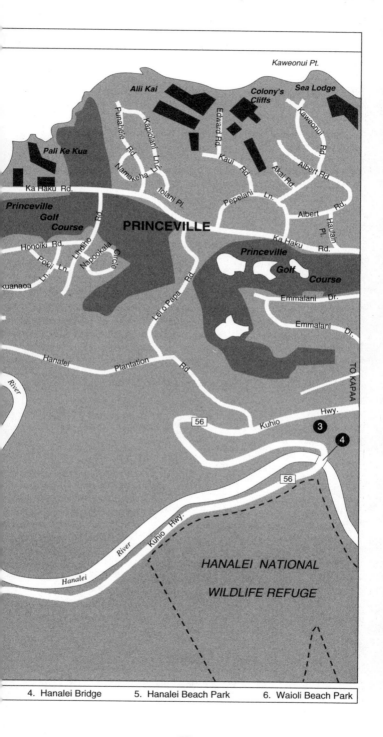

4. Hanalei Bridge   5. Hanalei Beach Park   6. Waioli Beach Park

Museum, housed in the former home of missionaries Abner and Lucy Wilcox. The Mission House, characteristic in its New England architecture, was originally built in 1837 — also by Reverend William P. Alexander and his wife — and restored in 1921 by the Wilcox' granddaughters, with the original missionary furnishings, dating from the late 1800s, including antique koa furniture as well as the original wood-burning stove and bookcases lined with several volumes from Abner Wilcox' collection. The museum is of course open to public viewing.

At Hanalei, too, bordering Hanalei Bay, is a 2-mile-long crescent-shaped beach, the Hanalei Pavillion Beach Park, quite popular with picnickers as well as with surfers for its gigantic swells in the winter months, reached by way of Aku Road which goes off the highway (560), *makai*, then Weke Road, which journeys along the periphery of the bay, with an access road on the right leading directly to the beach. From here, also, you can see the northeast portion of the spectacular Na Pali Coast, as well as Bali Hai, the spire-like ridge rising just to the west of Hanalei Bay, and enjoy some of the most beautiful sunsets on the island, over the bay.

Also of interest, northward on Weke Road, at the very end of the road, is the Black Pot Beach Park, situated at the mouth of the Hanalei River. Many of the cruise boats plying the Na Pali Coast depart from here, as well as kayaking trips, heading up the Hanalei River. Besides which, Black Pot Beach is an excellent place to watch sunsets and the waves, and the dramatic mountains that form a backdrop for the sleepy little town of Hanalei. The beach, interestingly, is named for a black cooking pot that was once a fixture here, especially useful on occasions when local residents would gather at the beach to fish and socialize — and add to the pot. There is also, by the way, a restored, 100-year-old pier at the beach, which was once used for loading bags of rice — grown in the valley — onto boats waiting in the bay, and which is now a popular place for pier fishing.

Try to also visit the Wai'oli Beach Park, also known as Pinetrees, reached by way of Weke Road south a mile or so from Black Pot Beach, to He'e Road, which goes off toward the ocean to the beach park. The beach, incidentally, located at an approximate midway point along the bay, is bordered by ironwoods, not pine trees, contrary to what its name might suggest. The beach, nevertheless, has good swimming possibilities in the summer months, when the ocean is calm; in winter and spring, however, the treacherous waves and dangerous rip tides make the area unsafe for the sport.

Westward on Highway 560, at mile marker 4, along the west side of Hanalei Bay is yet another beach, Waikoko Beach — a roadside beach, bordered by ironwood trees and protected from the open ocean by a coral reef, making it ideally suited to family recreation. The swimming area here, however, is much too shallow for adults, but safe and enjoyable for children.

Lumahai Beach to Ke'e Beach

West still, a mile past mile marker 4, then off on a trail toward the ocean, passing through groves of pandanus trees — also known as screw pines and, often enough, as "tourist pineapple trees" — lies Lumahai Beach, the most beautiful of Kauai's beaches, made famous by the movie, *South Pacific*, filmed on location here, in 1957. Lumahai, needless to say, is a very popular beach, three-quarters of a mile long, sandy, and with good swimming and snorkeling possibilities, at its eastern end, in the summer months, when the seas are calm. At the western end of the beach — where the Lumahai River drains into the ocean, and which is reached from the beach parking area, three quarter mile west of mile marker 5 on the Kuhio Highway (560) — surfing and bodysurfing, at advanced levels, are the dominant sports. There is also an overlook here, at mile marker 5, marked with a Hawaiian Visitors Bureau marker, with commanding views of Lumahai Beach.

West from Lumahai Beach, a half mile or so past mile marker 6, is the tiny village of Wainiha — meaning "unfriendly water" — the last place to obtain supplies before striking out farther west, toward Haena and the Na Pali Coast wilderness. West from Wainiha, too, another half mile, at mile marker 7, is Wainiha Beach, with its treacherous waters, where swimming is strongly discouraged.

Another nearby beach, Tunnels Beach, a rather popular beach, protected by a large reef and offering a variety of activities, depending on the season and prevailing ocean conditions, is located some 2 miles or so to the west of Wainiha — a half mile past mile marker 8 — with two separate access roads leading from the highway down to the beach. In calm weather, usually during the summer months, Tunnels Beach offers some of the best diving and snorkeling possibilities on the island; and in winter, when the ocean swells generate out-size waves, the area draws world-class surfers, to a point beyond the reef, known, simply, as "Tunnels." Tunnels Beach, we might add, is also well liked by windsurfers, when the winds are strong enough.

A quarter mile west of Tunnels Beach lies Haena Beach Park, with restrooms, showers and campsites, and largely unprotected from the ocean; and directly across from there, on the opposite side of the highway, is the Maniniholo Dry Cave, the first of three caves located alongside the highway here, a hundred yards

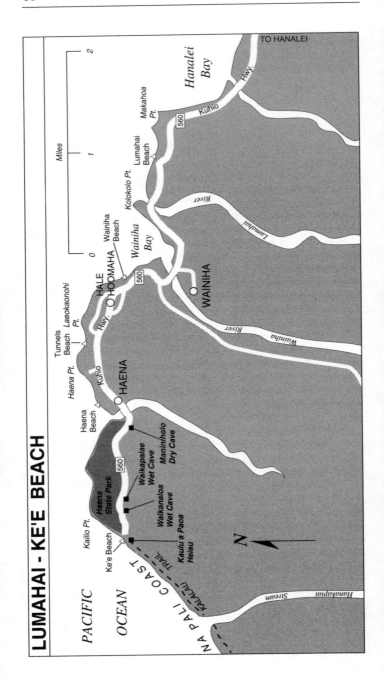

LUMAHAI - KE'E BEACH

deep, and with a large opening. The Maniniholo Cave, we are told, was dug out by hand, in ancient times, by a *menehune* fisherman searching for an evil spirit.

Westward from Haena Beach is the Haena State Park, encompassing all of 230 acres, and including in it, besides archaeological sites, the Waikanaloa and Waikapalae wet caves and Ke'e Beach. The Waikanaloa and Waikapalae caves, of course, are located just inside the park, on the *mauka* — inland — side of the highway, two-tenths and three-tenths of a mile from the park entrance, respectively. The caves, typically, are deep, dark, and large, dug out, apparently, by Pele, the Hawaiian goddess of fire, in her relentless search for fire. All she found in the caves, however, not surprisingly, was water. The caves, nevertheless, are now north shore landmarks, well visited.

At mile marker 10 — which is to say, approximately 8 miles from Hanalei, or 38 miles from Lihue — the road finally ends, at Ke'e Beach, a popular swimming and snorkeling beach — in calm seas, that is — protected from the ocean by a large coral reef. Ke'e Beach has showers and restroom facilities, and from its western end a trail journeys along the shoreline a little way, past the historic Allerton House — now a private residence — then up the hill to the ancient Ka'ulu a Paoa Heiau, situated in a grassy meadow, and dedicated to Laka, the goddess of the *hula*, where she, in fact, did much of her dancing. Dedicated students of the *hula* still make the pilgrimage to this ancient *heiau*, the most sacred shrine of the traditional Hawaiian dance of story-telling.

Nearby, at the Ke'e Beach parking lot is the Kalalau Trail trailhead, and just to its left, the site of the home of Lohiau, a legendary 16th century prince. It was here, we are told, that Pele, the goddess of fire, while searching for fire, was first distracted by the sound of the *hula* drums; and, upon seeing Lohiau, she instantly fell in love with him. But in her wisdom, she decided that she could not be his wife until she had found a suitable place to live; whereupon she continued her search, traveling to the other islands, finally settling in Kilauea, the mighty volcano in the center of the big island of Hawaii, where, indeed, she found fire. With that settled, Pele then sent her sister, Hi'iaka, to bring Lohiau to Kilauea; but upon her arrival at Lohiau's home, Hi'iaka found the prince dead. Nevertheless, not one to give up easily, Hi'iaka located Lohiau's spirit and brought him back to life, and the two departed for Kilauea. As they approached Kilauea, however, Hi'iaka, overjoyed at having accomplished her task, hugged and kissed Lohiau, the sight of which, naturally, sent Pele into a rage, and she ordered the death of Lohiau — to be buried in lava! But, as it turned out, two of Pele's brothers — kind-hearted souls — discovered Lohiau in the lava and rescued and brought him back to Kauai, where he was reunited with

Hi'iaka, and the two lived happily ever after — in Haena. The site of Lohiau's house can still be seen here, identified as a low rock terrace, receding into the mountains.

The Na Pali Coast

The Na Pali Coast is a spectacular, 15-mile coastal stretch along the northwestern end of the island — between Ke'e Beach and Polihale Beach — with steep, rugged cliffs plunging into the ocean, frequently overhung by ocean mist. The Na Pali Coast State Park, in fact, comprises some 6,000 acres of wild, un-spoiled coastal terrain, with lush, verdant valleys and dramatic sea cliffs, accessible only on foot, or by boat or helicopter — except during flash floods and high surf, when it becomes completely inaccessible.

The best way to see — or experience — the Na Pali Coast, of course, is on the rugged Kalalau Trail, which journeys from Ke'e Beach, winding some 11 miles along the wind- and wave-carved cliffs, to the ancient Kalalau Valley, at the ocean end of which lies the Kalalau Beach. The Kalalau Trail, however, we must point out, is a challenging, arduous hike — 8 to 10 hours each way — to be recommended only to the hardy souls. It is also possible to arrange for a drop off — or pick up — by boat, at Kalalau Beach, thus enabling adventurers to hike the trail just one way. Additionally, camping is permitted at Kalalau Beach — as well as at Hanakapiai Beach and the Hanakoa Valley, which lie to the northeast of Kalalau Beach — with camping permits available from the Department of Land and Natural Resources in Lihue.

In any case, for those journeying from the northeast end of the Na Pali Coast, the Kalalau Trail sets out from Ke'e Beach and heads directly southwest, climbing a mile or so, then de-scending another mile, approximately, to the delightful Ha-nakapiai Beach, which has some picnicking and camping possibilities. Here, also, just before reaching the Hanakapiai Beach, a trail dashes off inland, some 2 miles into the valley — passing by ancient rock-wall terraces, once used to cultivate *taro*, as well as a deserted coffee mill — to the picturesque Hanakapiai Falls, cascading some 250 feet over the cliffs, into a large pool, ideal for swimming. There are several other natural pools here, too, along the Hanakapiai Stream, all quite suitable for a refreshing little dip.

From Hanakapiai Beach, however, it is another 4 miles or so, climbing and weaving around a series of switchbacks, and passing through the Ho'olulu and Waiahuakua valleys along the way — 1 mile and 2½ miles from Hanakapiai Beach, respectively — to the lush, hanging Hanakoa Valley, which has camping possibilities as well as a handful of natural pools, dotted along the Hanakoa Stream, ideally suited to swimming. Here you can also visit the spectacular, 1,000-foot Hanakoa Falls, cascading in all their splendor into a large pool below, which, again, has good swimming possibilities. The falls are located roughly a third of a mile inside the valley, reached more or less directly on the trail leading into the valley.

Beyond Hanakoa Valley lies the Pohakuao Valley — comprising seven successive gulches — and some 5 miles from Hanakoa the Kalalau Trail finally ends, at Kalalau Beach — a secluded, sandy beach, approximately half mile long and some 80 yards wide, where, of course, camping is permitted, and where you can also view one or two large sea caves as well as a 100-foot-long 40-foot-wide *heiau*. From Kalalau Beach also, it is possible to hike inland a little way, into the Kalalau Valley, a deep, broad valley, surrounded by 3,000- to 4,000-foot cliffs, and notable, too, as the site of an ancient Hawaiian settlement, where native Hawaiians dwelled for centuries — until as recently as the 1920s! — with little or no contact with the outside world. Remnants of weathered rock-wall terraces are still visible here, once used by the ancient Hawaiians for cultivating *taro*. The valley, besides, is abundant in fruit trees — guava, papaya, mango — and kukui nut trees, and it also has in it a series of pools, ideal for swimming, and the 250-foot Waimakimaki Falls — also known as Davis Falls — reached on a mile-long trail from the site of the settlement. As added interest, the Kalalau Valley also provided the setting for the remake of the film, *King Kong*.

In the late 1800s, interestingly, the Kalalau Valley was also used as a hideout by a Hawaiian named Ko'olau. Ko'olau, we are told, having contracted leprosy, was sought out by the government for banishment to the leper colony on the remote Kalalau Peninsula on the island of Molokai. However, rather than be removed to the forlorn peninsula, Ko'olau fled with his wife and young son to the Kalalau Valley, where he eluded his captors for several years, until, finally, he and his son — who had, by then, also developed symptoms of the disease — died in hiding. Ko'olau's wife, Pi'ilani, then buried her husband and son and, in great sorrow, emerged from the valley.

In any event, from the Kalalau Valley, we must retrace our steps to Kalalau Beach and follow the Kalalau Trail northeastward to Hanakoa Valley, Hanakapiai Beach, and so to Ke'e Beach, our starting point.

PRACTICAL INFORMATION FOR KAUAI

HOW TO GET THERE

Kauai is the northernmost of the main Hawaiian islands, situated approximately 95 miles northwest of Oahu, and some $17\frac{1}{2}$ miles east of Ni'ihau. It can be reached directly from the U.S. mainland on regularly scheduled flights, or by way of Honolulu, Oahu, which is serviced by several different domestic as well as international airlines. Commercial flights arrive and depart at Kauai's *Lihue Airport*; commuter flights, between Honolulu and Kauai are also available to and from the island's *Princeville Airport*, located at Princeville, on Kauai's north shore.

Direct to Kauai

Direct flights from the U.S. mainland to Kauai are available on *United Airlines* (800) 241-6522. For a schedule and fare information, contact the airline.

Via Honolulu

Domestic Airlines. The following domestic airlines service the Honolulu Airport: *American Airlines* (800) 433-7300; *America West* (800) 247-5692; *Continental Airlines* (800) 525-0280; *Delta Air Lines* (800) 221-1212; *Hawaiian Airlines* (800) 882-8811; *Northwest Airlines* (800) 225-2525; and *United Airlines* (800) 241-6522.

International Airlines. The following international airlines offer scheduled flights to Honolulu: *Air New Zealand* (800) 262-1234; *Canadian Airlines International* (800) 426-7000; *China Airlines* (808) 536-6951; *Japan Air Lines* (800) 232-2517; *Korea Air* (808) 923-7302; *Philippines Airlines* (800) 435-9725; and *Singapore Airlines* (808) 542-6063.

Honolulu to Kauai

The following airlines offer regular, scheduled inter-island flights between Honolulu, Oahu, and Kauai: *Aloha Airlines* (808) 244-9071; *Aloha Island Air* (800) 652-6541; and *Hawaiian Airlines* (800) 882-8811. Fares, typically, range from $49-$99 one-way, to $98-$138 round-trip.

Lumahai Beach enjoys a picture-perfect setting on the north shore

Eroded mountains in the Waimea Canyon

Taro patches in the Hanalei Valley

Fern Grotto, one of the island's most popular attractions

TOURIST INFORMATION

Hawaii Visitors Bureau (HVB) - Kauai. 3016 Umi St., Lihue, HI 96766; (808) 245-3971. Wealth of tourist information available, including directory of accommodations and restaurants and a calendar of events. Also maps, and a tourist publication, *The Islands of Hawaii: A Vacation Planner*, covering places of interest on the islands, recreation and tours. The *Hawaii Visitors Bureau* also maintains offices at the following locations: *HVB Main Office,* Waikiki Business Plaza, 2270 Kalakaua Ave., Suite 808, Honolulu, HI 96815, (808) 923-1811; *HVB Los Angeles,* 3440 Wilshire Blvd., Suite 502, CA 90010, (213) 385-5301; *HVB San Francisco,* 50 California St., Suite 450, San Francisco, CA 94111, (415) 392-8173.

Kauai Chamber of Commerce. 2970 Kele, Room 201, Lihue, HI 96766; (808) 245-7363. Visitor information brochures, including lodging, restaurant and tour company listings.

Publications. There are also several free publications available on the island, at airports, hotels, restaurants and shopping centers, with valuable tourist information and articles of local interest. The following are among the best-known — the *Drive Guide*, published three times a year and available at rental car agencies, offers information on dining, island activities and sightseeing, and includes maps; *Kauai Beach Press*, published weekly on Mondays, features up-to-date information on dining, entertainment, activities and island adventures, and also contains an island map and discount coupons; *Spotlight Kauai*, a monthly magazine, offers tips on dining, shopping, fun activities and sightseeing, with maps and coupons; and *This Week Kauai*, a weekly magazine, contains information on activities on the island, and shopping, dining and sightseeing, as well as maps and discount coupons.

HOW TO GET AROUND

By Car. Rental cars are available from several different car rental agencies on the island. Rental rates for sub-compacts to larger luxury cars range from $18-$70 per day to $90-$350 per week. Some of the companies also offer four-wheel-drive vehicles, especially useful if you plan to visit some of the more remote parts of the island. For rentals, availability and more information, contact any of the following: *Alamo,* Lihue Airport, (808) 246-0645/(800) 327-9633; *Avis,* Lihue Airport, (808) 245-3512/(800) 321-3712, and at Princeville Airport, (808) 826-9773/(800) 831-8000; *Budget,* Lihue Airport, (808) 245-1901/(800) 527-0700; *Dollar,* Lihue Airport, (808) 245-3651/(800) 800-4000; *Hertz,* Lihue Airport, (808) 245-3356/(800) 654-3131, and at the Princeville Airport, (808) 826-7455; *National,* Lihue Airport, (808) 245-5636/(800) 227-7368; or *Thrifty,* Lihue Airport, (808) 833-

0046/(800) 367-2277.

By Taxi. The following taxi companies service the island: *ABC TAXI,* (808) 822-7641; *Aloha Taxi,* (808) 245-4609; *Al's Koloa-Poipu VIP Taxicabs,* (808) 742-1390; *Hanamaulu Taxi,* (808) 245-3727; *Kauai Cab Service,* (808) 246-9554; *Lorenzo's Taxi Service,* (808) 245-6331; *North Shore Cab & Tours,* (808) 826-6189. Taxi fares from Lihue Airport, typically, are $30 to Poipu, $15-$20 to Kapa'a, $55-$60 to Princeville, and $65-$70 to Hanalei.

ACCOMMODATIONS

(Reservations for accommodations on Kauai can be made centrally through *Kauai 800,* P.O. Box 640, Koloa, HI 96756, (808) 742-7989/(800) 443-9180.)

Lihue

Aston Kauai Beach Villas. *$100-$255.* 4330 Kauai Beach Dr., Lihue; (808) 245-7711/(800) 922-7866. 150-unit condominium complex, located on the beach. Phones, TV, kitchenettes, and air conditioning. Swimming pool, tennis court.

Banyan Harbor Resort. *$95-$105.* 3411 Wilcox Rd., Lihue; (808) 245-7333/(800) 422-6926. 148 two-bedroom condominium units, with TV, phones, and full kitchen and laundry facilities. Swimming pool and tennis court on premises.

Garden Island Inn. *$50-$85.* 3445 Wilcox Rd., Lihue; (808) 245-7227/(800) 648-0154. 21 units with TV, refrigerators, microwave ovens, coffee makers, and ceiling fans.

Kaha Lani. *$120-$250.* 4460 Nehe Rd., Lihue; (808) 822-9331/(800) 922-7866. Oceanfront condominium complex, with 65 one-, two- and three-bedroom units. TV, phones, full kitchens, laundry facilities. Also swimming pool, tennis courts and barbecue area.

Outrigger Kauai Beach. *$110-$380.* 4331 Kauai Beach Dr., Lihue; (808) 245-1955/(800) 462-6262. Beachfront hotel with 350 units with TV, phones and air conditioning. Swimming pool, spa, tennis court, restaurant and cocktail lounge, meeting rooms, shops and beauty salon. Handicapped facilities.Complimentary continental breakfast.

Tip Top Motel. *$30-$39.* 3173 Akahi St., Lihue; (808) 245-2333. 34 units, with TV, and air conditioning. Bakery, restaurant and cocktail lounge on premises.

Kauai Marriott. *$195-$395.* Kalapaki Beach, Lihue; (808) 245-5050/(800) 228-9290. Rambling, luxury resort, with 335 rooms and suites, situated on the beach. Facilities include an expansive swimming pool, health club and spas, and tennis courts. Also restaurants and cocktail lounges, meeting rooms, and two shopping villages on premises.

South Shore

Colony's Lawai Beach Resort. *$125-$185.* 5017 Lawai Rd., Poipu; (808) 742-9581/(800) 777-1700. 61 condominium units with ocean views. TV, phones, kitchens, and daily maid service. Swimming pool. Handicapped facilities.

Colony's Poipu Kai Resort. *$150-$325.* 1941 Poipu Rd., Poipu; (808) 742-6464/(800) 777-1700. 112 condominium units with ocean and garden views; TV, phones, kitchens, and daily maid service. Swimming pools; swimming pool. Weekly maid service. Minimum stay, restaurant and cocktail lounge on premises; also meeting room available.

Garden Isle Cottages. *$49-$80.* 2666 Pu'uholo Rd., Koloa; (808) 742-6717. 9 oceanfront cottages, overlooking Koloa Landing. TV in cottages; swimming pool. Weekly maid service. Minimum stay, 2 days.

Hale Hoku. *$150-$230.* 4534 Lawai Rd., Koloa; (808) 742-1509. Oceanfront condominium; two-bedroom unit with TV, VCR, phones, full kitchen, and laundry facilities. Also barbecue area on premises.

Hyatt Regency Kauai. *$230-$345.* 1571 Poipu Rd., Poipu; (808) 742-1234/(800) 233-1234. Luxury hotel, located on the beach. 600 rooms and suites, with TV, phones and air conditioning. Swimming pools, health club and spa, tennis courts and golf course. Shops, restaurants, cocktail lounges, and meeting rooms. Handicapped facilities.

Kiahuna Plantation. *$150-$380.* 2253 Poipu Rd., Poipu; (808) 742-6411/(800) 367-7052. 333 condominium units, with TV, phones and kitchens. Swimming pool, tennis courts, restaurant and cocktail lounge. Daily maid service. Handicapped facilities. Minimum stay, 2 days.

Koloa Landing Cottages. *$50-$100.* 2704B Hoonani Rd., Koloa; (808) 742-1470. Studio units, self-contained cottages and one 2-bedroom house available for rental; TV and phones, full kitchens. Minimum stay, 2 days.

Nihi Kai Villas. *$99-$250.* 1870 Hoone Rd., Poipu; (808) 742-1412/(800) 742-1412/(800) 325-5701. 70 one-, two- and three-bedroom condominium units, most with ocean views. TV, phones, laundry facilities. Swimming pool and tennis court.

Poipu Kai Resort. *$100-$345.* 1941 Poipu Rd., Koloa; (800) 688-2254. 350-unit condominium complex. TV, phones, and private lanais; some ocean views, some garden views. Swimming pool, spa, tennis court. Also restaurant and cocktail lounge on premises.

Poipu Kapili. *$150-$350.* 2221 Kapili Rd., Koloa; (808) 742-6449/(800) 443-7714. 60 one- and two-bedroom condominium units, with TV, VCR and phones. Swimming pool, tennis courts.

Poipu Plantation. *$80-$90.* 1792-A Pe'e Rd., Poipu; (808) 742-6757/(800) 733-1632. 9 plantation-style units, with ocean and garden views, located within easy distance of Poipu Beach. TV, phones, ceiling fans, and kitchens; also library and laundry for guests' use.

Poipu Shores. *$135-$200.* 1755 Pe'e Rd., Koloa; (808) 742-7700. 39 oceanfront condominiums units, with one, two and three bedrooms. TV, phones, full kitchens; swimming pool and barbecue area.

Prince Kuhio Resort. *$60-$95.* 5160 Lawai Rd., Koloa; (808) 245-4711/(800) 767-4707. 65 condominium units, close to beach. TV, phones, kitchen facilities, swimming pool.

Sheraton Kauai Garden Hotel. *$95-$350.* 2440 Hoonani Rd.,

Poipu; (808) 742-1661/(808) 742-2442/(800) 325-3535. Full-service resort hotel, with 230 units. TV, phones, and air conditioning. Swimming pool, tennis courts, restaurants and cocktail lounge, meeting rooms, beauty salon. Handicapped facilities.

Waikomo Stream Villas. *$79-$120.* 2721 Poipu Rd., Poipu; (808) 742-7220/(800) 325-5701. 31 condominium units with TV, phones, and kitchens. Swimming pool and tennis court. Maid service available upon request. Minimum stay, 3 days.

Whaler's Cove. *$275-$325.* 2640 Pu'uholo Rd., Koloa; (808) 742-7571/(800) 367-7052. 28 condominium units with garden and ocean views. TV, phones, ceiling fans and kitchen. Daily maid service. Minimum stay is 2 nights.

West Side

Kokee Lodge. *$35-$45.* Located in the Kokee State Park, on Kokee Rd., 13 miles north of Waimea; (808) 335-6061. 12 cabins with kitchens. Restaurant and cocktail lounge, and shops nearby. Maximum stay, 5 days.

Waimea Plantation Cottages. *$65-$200.* 9600 Kaumuali'i Hwy., #367, Waimea; (808) 338-1625/(800) 9-WAIMEA. 46 units, located on the beach. TV, phones, kitchens; swimming pool. Handicapped facilities. Minimum stay, 3 days.

East Side

Aston Kauai Beachboy. *$88-$118.* 4-484 Kuhio Hwy., Kapa'a; (808) 822-3441/(800) 922-7866. 243 units; TV, phones, air conditioning. Swimming pool, tennis courts, restaurants and cocktail lounge; also meeting rooms, and shops on premises.

Coco Palms Resort. *$110-$160.* 4-241 Kuhio Hwy., Wailua; (808) 823-0760/822-4921/(800) 338-1338. 390 units, with phones, TV, and air conditioning. Swimming pools, tennis courts, restaurant and cocktail lounge, meeting rooms, shops and beauty salon. Handicapped facilities. Located across from Wailua Beach.

Colony's Lae Nani. *$150-$250.* 410 Papaloa Rd., Kapa'a; (808) 822-4938/(800) 777-1700. 84 beachfront condominium units, with TV, phones, ceiling fans and kitchens. Swimming pool, tennis court. Daily maid service. Handicapped facilities.

Hotel Coral Reef. *$50-$85.* 1516 Kuhio Hwy., Kapa'a; (808) 822-4481/(800) 843-4659. 25 units in beachfront hotel. TV, phones; complimentary breakfast. Handicapped facilities.

Islander on the Beach. *$95-$185.* 484 Kuhio Hwy., Kapa'a; (808) 822-7417/(800) 847-7417. Oceanfront hotel with 198 units, some with ocean views and some with garden views. TV, phones, refrigerators, wet bars, air conditioning, private balconies. Also swimming pool, restaurant and cocktail lounge, and shops.

Kapa'a Sands Resort. *$75-$109.* 380 Papaloa Rd., Kapa'a; (808)

822-4901/(800) 222-4901. 24 oceanfront condominium units, including studios and 2-bedroom units. TV, phones; swimming pool.

Kauai Coconut Beach Hotel. *$115-$215.* At the Coconut Plantation (P.O. Box 830), Kapa'a; (808) 822-3455/(800) 222-5642. Oceanfront hotel, with 308 units with TV, phones, and air conditioning. Swimming pool, tennis courts, restaurant and cocktail lounge, meeting rooms, shops. Handicapped facilities.

Kauai Resort Hotel. *$99-$200.* 3-5920 Kuhio Hwy., Kapa'a; (808) 245-3931/(800) 367-5004, (800) 272-5275 in Hawaii. 242 beachfront units, with TV, room phones and air conditioning. Swimming pool, tennis court, restaurant and cocktail lounge, and shops. Handicapped facilities.

Plantation Hale. *$105-120.* 484 Kuhio Hwy., Kapa'a; (808) 822-4941/(800) 775-4253. 152 units in beachfront condominium complex. TV, phones, air conditioning and kitchen facilities. Swimming pool; also restaurant and cocktail lounge, and shops nearby.

Pono Kai. *$115-$175.* 1250 Kuhio Hwy., Kapa'a; (808) 822-9831/(800) 438-6493. 217-unit beachfront condominium complex, with one- and two-bedroom units. TV, phones, kitchens, and laundry facilities. Swimming pool, spa, sauna, tennis courts, shuffleboard; also barbecue area.

Rosewood. *$55-$100.* 872 Kamalu Rd., Kapa'a; (808) 822-5216. Restored macadamia nut plantation estate, with condominium units, bed and breakfast accommodations and a self-contained cottage. TV and phones. All non-smoking units.

Sleeping Giant International. *$15-$40.* 4534 Kehua St., Kapa'a; (808) 823-6142/823-8068. Guest house and hostel, with 30 dormitory units and 4 private units. Shared kitchen, bathroom, TV and phone. Daily island excursions offered.

Wailua Bay View Condominiums. *$115-$125.* 320 Papaloa Rd., Kapa'a; (808) 391-8932/822-3651/(800) 225-7978. 40 one-bedroom oceanfront condominium units, with TV, phones, microwave ovens and laundry facilities; some with air-conditioning. Swimming pool and barbecue area.

North Shore

Alii Kai I and II. *$110-$250.* 3830 Edwards Rd., Princeville; (808) 826-9988/826-7444//(800) 648-9988/(800) 222-5541. Oceanfront condominium complex with two-bedroom units with TV and phones. Restaurant and cocktail lounge on premises; also swimming pool, spa and health club. Golf course nearby.

Colony's Cliffs at Princeville. *$120-$195.* 3811 Edwards Rd., Princeville; (808) 826-6219/(800) 367-7052/(800) 777-1700. 172 units, overlooking ocean; TV, phones, kitchenettes. Swimming pool, health club and spa, tennis courts, golf course. Also restaurant, and meeting rooms. Handicapped facilities.

Hale Makai Beach Cottages. *$125-$165.* P.O. Box 1109, Hanalei, HI 96714; (808) 826-7288/(800) 487-9833. 4 beachfront cottages, with TV and phones, and maid service upon request. Minimum stay, 3 days.

Hale Moi. *$95-$145.* 5300 Ka Haku Rd., Princeville; (808) 826-9602/(800) 535-0085. 40 condominium units with TV and phones; most with kitchens. Suites, studios and one-bedroom units available, with mountain and garden views.

Hanalei Bay Resort. *$130-$460.* 5380 Honoiki Rd., Princeville; (808) 826-6522/(800) 827-4427. 85 one- and two-bedroom units, with TV, phones, and air conditioning. Swimming pools, tennis courts, shops and beauty salon. Restaurants and cocktail lounge; meeting rooms. Handicapped facilities.

Hanalei Bay Villas. *$125-$200.* 5451 Honoiki Rd., Princeville; (808) 826-6585/(800) 222-5541. 40 one- and two-bedroom units, with TV, phones, and full kitchens. Located on bluff overlooking Hanalei Bay.

Hanalei Colony Resort. *$95-$190.* P.O. Box 206, Hanalei, HI 96722; (808) 826-6235/(800) 628-3004. Oceanfront condominium complex with 46 rental units with garden and ocean views, and kitchen facilities. Swimming pool on premises. Minimum stay, 3 days.

Mauna Kai. *$95-$145.* P.O. Box 1109, Hanalei, HI 96714; (808) 826-7288/(800) 487-9833. 46 condominium units with TV and phones. Swimming pool.

Pali Ke Kua. *$80-$185.* 5300 Ka Haku Rd., Princeville; (808) 922-9700/826-9066/(800) 535-0085. 98-unit oceanfront condominium complex, offering suites and one- and two-bedroom units. TV, phones, full kitchens. Swimming pool and spa; restaurant.

Princeville Hotel. *$225-$495.* 5520 Kahaku Rd., Princeville; (808) 826-9644/(800) 826-4400. Full-fledged, luxury resort hotel, with 252 rooms and suites, overlooking Hanalei Bay. Hotel facilities include a swimming pool, spa, health club, tennis courts, golf courses, restaurants and cocktail lounges, meeting rooms, shops and beauty salon, and an in-house cinema. Handicapped facilities.

Puamana. *$105-$145.* P.O. Box 1109, Hanalei, HI 96714; (808) 826-7288/826-9768/(800) 487-9833. 98 condominium units with TV, phones and full kitchens. Swimming pool.

Pu'u Po'a. *$185-$225.* 5300 Ka Haku Rd., Princeville; (808) 922-9700/826-9602/(800) 535-0085. Oceanfront condominium complex with 56 two-bedroom units with TV and phones. Swimming pool, tennis courts.

Sandpiper Village. *$95-$175.* 4770 Pepelani Loop, Princeville; (808) 826-6585/826-8613/(800) 222-5541. 148 condominium units, located close to Princeville golf course. Swimming pool, spa and health club on premises.

Sea Lodge. *$95-$125.* P.O. Box 1109, Hanalei, HI 96714; (808) 826-7288/826-6751/(800) 487-9833. 87-unit oceanfront condominium complex. TV, phones; swimming pool.

BED & BREAKFAST INNS

(Reservations for bed and breakfast inns on the island can be made centrally through *All Islands Bed & Breakfast*, 823 Kainui Dr., Kailua, (808) 236-2342/(800) 542-0344; *Bed & Breakfast Hawaii*, P.O. Box 449, Kapa'a, (808) 822-7771/(800) 733-1632; or *Bed & Breakfast Wailua*, 6436 Kalama Rd., Kapa'a, (808) 822-1177/(800) 822-1176.)

South Shore

Classic Vacation Cottages. *$60-$70*. 2687 Onu Place, Kalaheo; (808) 332-9201. 4 self-contained cottages, with TV and kitchens; situated in rural, country surroundings, not far from the South Shore beaches. Daily maid service. Continental breakfast available for an additional charge of around $5.00. Minimum stay, 2 days.

Gloria's Spouting Horn Bed & Breakfast. *$125-$150*. 4464 Lawai Rd., Poipu; (808) 742-6995. Tropical beach house. 4 guest rooms with shared and private baths; also ceiling fans, refrigerators, and TV and phones in rooms. Maid service on request. Continental breakfast. Minimum stay, 3 days.

Marjorie's. *$65-$75*. 3307-D Hailima Rd., Lawai; (808) 332-8838/(800) 443-9180. Situated on 1-acre property, with views of Lawai Valley. Offers 2 guest rooms with private baths and lanais; also in-room TV and phone, microwave oven, and refrigerator. Outdoor hot tub and spa, in gazebo.

Poipu Bed & Breakfast Inn. *$95-$175*. 2720 Hoonani Rd., Poipu; (808) 742-1146/(800) 552-0095/(800) 22-POIPU. Restored, 1933 plantation home, located one block from the beach. 9 rooms with private baths; TV and phones, refrigerators, ceiling fans. Swimming pool, tennis court. Tropical continental breakfast, and afternoon tea.

Tally's Hale Mahiko Bed & Breakfast. *$60-$125*. 4122 Koloa Rd., Lawai; (808) 332-9164/(800) 808-9251. Old, plantation-style home, nestled amid lush, tropical plants, and decorated with 18th-century furniture from Jerome, Arizona. 3 guest rooms, with refrigerators; also private baths. Continental breakfast, consisting of fresh fruit and juice, coffee, tea, and homemade muffins.

Victoria Place Bed & Breakfast Inn. *$75-$105*. 3459 Lawai Loa Ln., Koloa; (808) 332-9300. 4 guest rooms, including 3 with shared baths and 1 studio with private entrance. TV and phones; parlor, library, swimming pool. Full breakfast. Quiet setting.

East Side

Alohilani Bed & Breakfast. *$85-$95*. 1470 Wanaao Rd., Kapa'a; (808) 823-0128. Pastoral setting; views of ocean, cane fields and Mt. Wai'ale'ale. 3 guest rooms, with TV, phones and ceiling fans. Private lanais, kitchens; gazebo and outdoor hot pool. "Aloha Breakfast," featuring locally-grown fruit and homemade muffins. Located close to beach.

Aleva House. *$50-$55*. 5509 Kuamoo Rd., Kapa'a; (808) 822-4606.

Rural home located near Opaekaa Falls. 2 rooms with shared bath. Hosts knowledgeable in Hawaiian mythology and folklore.

Anahola Beach Club. *$65-$85.* 4023 Anahola Rd., Anahola; (808) 822-6966. Situated on Anahola Beach, surrounded by tropical flowers. 4 units with private baths and sun decks; living room decorated in South Pacific-style. Full breakfast, and complimentary refreshments at sunset.

Bed & Breakfast — Kauai Calls. *$50-$75.* 5972 Heamoi Pl., Kapa'a; (808) 822-9699/(800) 522-9699. 2 comfortable guest rooms, with TV, refrigerator, microwave oven, ceiling fan, and hot tub. Private baths. Daily maid service. Minimum stay, 3 days.

Fern Grotto Inn. *$80-$100.* 4561 Kuamoo Rd., Wailua; (808) 822-2560. Plantation home, located along the Wailua River. 3 rooms with private baths; feather beds. Hearty tropical breakfast, including fresh breads and homemade cereals, freshly squeezed fruit juice, and Kona coffee.

Ikena Nani Loa Bed & Breakfast. *$50-$75.* 139 Royal Dr., Wailua; (808) 822-4010. Ikena Nani Loa, meaning "magnificent views," is named for its superb views of Wailua Valley and Mt. Wai'ale'ale. The mini retreat comprises six rental units, including individual rooms, a cottage and a townhouse. Swimming pool on premises. Breakfast features island fruit, fresh juice, coffee, and homemade muffins and cereal.

Kay Barker's Bed & Breakfast. *$45-$70.* Ki'ilani Pl., Wailua; (808) 822-3073/(800) 835-2845. 5 rooms with private baths in large house; picture windows, overlooking gardens and pastures. Continental breakfast includes fresh fruit and pastries, and coffee and selection of tea.

Keapana Center Bed & Breakfast. *$50-$75.* 5620 Keapana Rd., Kapa'a; (808) 822-7968/(800) 822-7968. Large home in quiet, mountain setting, surrounded by lush gardens and pasture lands. 4 guest rooms with shared and private baths. Also jacuzzi. Continental breakfast, served on an open lanai. 2-day minimum stay.

Lampy's Bed & Breakfast. *$45-$55.* 6078 Kolopua St., Kapa'a; (808) 822-0478/(800) 777-1700. 4-room home, situated on half-acre estate, amid landscaped gardens. Private baths. Continental breakfast, consisting of fresh juice and island fruit, and homemade pastries and muffins. 2-day minimum stay.

Mohala Ke Ola. *$75-$105.* 5663 Ohelo Rd., Kapa'a; (808) 823-6398. 2 guest rooms with mountain views; TV, phones, private baths. Swimming pool; jacuzzi. Full breakfast.

Winters Macnut Farm & Inn. *$50-$125.* 6470 Makana Rd., Wailua; (808) 822-3470/(800) 572-8156. Set on a macadamia nut farm. 5 rooms with private baths and kitchens, and one private home. Delightful lanai, with views of waterfalls. Breakfast consists of locally grown fruit and freshly baked muffins and pastries. 3-day minimum stay.

North Shore

Hale-Aha. *$80-$190.* 3875 Kamehameha Rd., Princeville; (808) 826-6733/(800) 826-6733. Lovely setting, on the golf course, with views of the ocean. 4 guest rooms, decorated in soft pastels; TV, refrigerators, private baths. Continental breakfast; maid service on request. Minimum stay, 3 days.

Hale Hoo Maha. *$55-$70.* 4041 Ka'iana Rd., Princeville; (808) 826-1130. 2 rooms with private baths; ocean and mountain views. Spacious living room, and fully-equipped kitchen for guests' use. Continental breakfast, featuring homemade delicacies.

Tassa Hanalei. *$75-$95.* P.O. Box 856, Hanalei, HI 96714; (808) 826-7298. Hawaiian-style recreation of Tassajara Hot Springs resort in Big Sur, California. Lovely setting, amid lush, tropical plants, near the Wainiha River. 3 rooms with private baths. Hot tub.

VACATION RENTALS

Anini Beach Vacation Rentals. P.O. Box 1220, Hanalei, HI 96714; (808) 826-4000/(800) 448-6333. Two-, three- and four-bedroom homes in the Hanalei and Princeville areas; also rental homes in other parts of the island. Rentals range from $500 to $3,600 per week. Minimum stay: 4 nights.

Blue Water Vacation Rentals. P.O. Box 366, Princeville, HI 96722; (808) 826-9229/(800) 628-5533. Condominium units and homes, one to four bedrooms, with ocean and golf course views, located at the Princeville Resort. Weekly rates: $500-$5,000. Minimum stay, 3 nights.

Garden Island Rentals. P.O. Box 57, Koloa, HI 96756; (808) 742-9537/(800) 247-5599. One- to five-bedroom homes and condominium units in the Poipu area, many situated on the beach, with ocean views. Daily rental rates begin at $75; weekly rates, $500-$3,200.

Grantham Resorts. 2721 Poipu Rd., Koloa, HI 96756; (808) 742-7220/(800) 325-5701. One- to four-bedroom condominium units and houses, both beachfront and with ocean views, located in the Poipu Beach area. Daily rates from $120-$220; weekly rates from $700-$1950. Minimum stay: 3 nights.

Hanalei Aloha Rental Management. P.O. Box 1109, Hanalei, HI 96714; (808) 826-7288/(800) 487-9833. One- to four-bedroom condominiums and homes at the Princeville Resort; ocean and golf course views. Rentals range from $65 to $170 per day. Minimum stay, 3 nights.

Kauai Paradise Vacations. P.O. Box 1622, Hanalei, HI 96714; (808) 826-7444/(800) 826-7782. One-, two- and three-bedroom homes and condominium units in Princeville, with ocean views. Rentals range from $100-$225 per day to $650-$1,575 per week.

Kauai Vacation Rentals. P.O. Box 3194, Lihue, HI 96766; (808) 245-8841/(800) 367-5025. One- to four-bedroom condominium units and homes, on Kauai's North, East and South shores; many beachfront and oceanview properties. Rental rates range from $90-$560 per day to $450-$2,800 per week.

Mark Resorts. P.O. Box 899, Hanalei, HI 96714; (808) 826-9066/(800) 535-0085. One- and two-bedroom condominium units in the Princeville area, with mountain and ocean views, ranging from $135-$225 per day to $720-$1,230 per week.

Na Pali Properties. P.O. Box 475, Hanalei, HI 96714; (808) 826-

7272/822-7774. One- to five-bedroom homes and condominiums, located on the North Shore of Kauai. Several beachfront properties. Rentals range from $450-$3,150 per week.

North Shore Properties. P.O. Box 607, Hanalei, HI 96714; (808) 826-9622/(800) 488-3336. One- to four-bedroom homes and condominiums on Kauai's North Shore; ocean and mountain views. Weekly rates: $500-$5,000.

Oceanfront Realty. P.O. Box 3570, Princeville, HI 96722; (808) 826-6585/(800) 222-5541. One- to four-bedroom condominium units in Princeville, with ocean, mountain and golf course views. Daily rates: $80-$395.

Prosser Realty, Inc. P.O. Box 367, 4379 Rice St., Lihue, HI 96766; (808) 245-4711/(800) 767-4707. One-, two- and three-bedroom homes and condominium units, located throughout the island; ocean and mountain views. Daily rates: $90-$175; weekly rates: $540-$3,000.

R & R Realty & Rentals. 1661 Pe'e Rd., Poipu, HI 96756; (808) 742-7555/(800) 367-8022. One- and two-bedroom homes and condominium units, with ocean and mountain views, located in the Poipu Beach area. Rentals range from $100-$225 per day to $665-$1,400 per week. Minimum stay: 4 nights.

SEASONAL EVENTS

March

Third Weekend. *Prince Kuhio Ironwoman Canoe Race* and *Prince Kuhio Ironman Canoe Race*. Popular annual events. The races begin at Hanama'ulu Beach and end at Wailua Beach and the Kalapaki Beach at the Westin Kauai Hotel, respectively. Party after the races, with food and live entertainment, including music and hula dancers. For more information on the races, call (808) 245-3971. *Prince Kuhio Run.* 5K and 10K runs, drawing nearly 100 participants. Races begin at Prince Kuhio Park on the south shore, and end at the Poipu Shopping Village in Poipu. More information on (808) 742-9511.

April

First Weekend. *Buddha Day.* Celebration of the birth of Buddha, with Buddhist festivities, including flower pageants, staged at Buddhist temples throughout the islands. For more information, call (808) 536-7044.

May

First Weekend. *Lei Day.* Celebration of Hawaiian leis, with an island-wide lei-making competition, held at the Kauai Museum in Lihue. Features colorful leis, made from flowers, feathers and shells; also crowning of Lei Queen. (808) 245-6931.

Fourth Weekend. *Taste of Hawaii.* Chefs from all the Hawaiian islands offer their favorite foods for sampling. Also live musical entertainment. For more information and location of events, call (808) 822-4904.

June

Second Weekend. *Kamehameha Day.* Celebration honoring Hawaii's first great monarch, King Kamehameha I, held on June 11 each year. Several hotels around the island participate, hosting hula competitions, a Hawaiian ball and costume competitions, and Hawaiian get-togethers with Hawaiian food and games and traditional Hawaiian music. Also colorful parade with floral floats, beginning at the Vidinha Stadium and ending at the County Building in Lihue. For more information, call (808) 245-8271.

July

First Week. *July 4th Concert in the Sky.* Held at the Vidinha Stadium, Lihue. Elaborate fireworks display. Also arts and crafts, food concessions, musical entertainment, and a variety of carnival games and activities.

Third Weekend. *Koloa Plantation Days.* Week-long celebration, commemorating the birth of Hawaii's sugar industry in Koloa. Features a parade through the town of Koloa, as well as a classic car show, lecture on the history of Old Koloa Town, and entertainment, including ethnic songs and dances. Also arts and crafts fair, and food concessions. For a schedule of events, call (808) 332-9201.

August

Second Weekend. *Kauai Tahiti Fete.* Held at the Kukui Park and Pavilion, in Lihue. Tahitian dance and drumming competition, featuring 10 different groups of performers and some 150 soloists. Also hula and Hawaiian music entertainment, Polynesian arts and crafts, and food concessions. (808) 823-0785.

September

First Weekend. *Kauai County Farm Fair.* Held at the Kauai War Memorial Convention Hall, Lihue. Features farm exhibits, livestock, produce and flowers; also carnival rides, and food concessions. For more information, call (808) 241-3471.

Third Weekend. *Mokihana Festival.* 10-day Hawaiiana festival, celebrated throughout the island. Features songs, hula competition, and a walking art gallery displaying works of local artists. For more information and a schedule of events, call (808) 822-0426.

October

First Weekend. *Kauai Loves You Triathlon.* Kalapaki Bay, Lihue. Popular event, drawing nearly 500 participants from all over the world. Course includes 1.5-mile swim, 54-mile bicycle ride and 12.4-mile run, beginning and ending at Kalapaki Bay. For more information, call (800) 247-9201 or (808) 826-9343.

Third Week. *Aloha Week.* Week-long festival, with events staged throughout the island, at Kapa'a, Hanalei, Coco Palms Resort, Kalapaki Bay and Koloa. Features a variety of Hawaiian pageantry and demonstrations in lei making, poi pounding, coconut husking, coconut weaving and Hawaiian style of quilting. Also parades, arts and crafts, food, island fruit tasting, canoe races, and entertainment — including original Hawaiian music and hula dancers. For a schedule of events and more information, call the Hawaii Visitors Bureau at (808) 245-3971. *Waimea Town Celebration.* Held at the festival fairgrounds in Waimea. Annual celebration; attracts nearly 10,000 people. Festivities include games, crafts, musical entertainment and hula dancers, food concessions, canoe races, parades with floats, marching bands and equestrian units. Also features 2K, 5K and 10K fun runs through the town of Waimea, and mountain bike races, pumpkin carving contest, mule race, and a Halloween costume contest. For a schedule of events and more information, call (808) 338-1316. *Taro Festival.* At the Waioli Park, Hanalei. Arts and crafts, food concessions, cooking demonstrations, and a variety of entertainment. Also educational exhibits and displays, Hawaiian children's games, and auction. More information on (808) 826-6522.

November

Second Weekend. *PGA Grand Slam.* Held at the Poipu Bay Resort Golf Course, adjacent to the Hyatt Regency, in Poipu. World-class, professional golfers vie for a $1 million prize. More information on (808) 742-6236. *International Film Festival.* Variety of international films, shown at theaters throughout the island. For a schedule, call (808) 246-2111.

Third Weekend. *Savor the Flavors of Kauai.* At the Prince Clubhouse, in Princeville. Features some 35 booths where Kauai producers offer a variety of local fruit, coffee, and also crafts. Also several Kauai restaurants offer their favorite recipes to the public for sampling. Live music, including Hawaiian, jazz and contemporary, and hula presentations. For more information, call (808) 826-9343.

December

First Weekend. *Kauai Museum Craft Fair.* At the Kauai Museum in Lihue. Features locally-made crafts. (808) 245-6931.

PLACES OF INTEREST

Lihue

Grove Farm Homestead. Nawiliwili Rd., Lihue; (808) 245-3202. Authentic, wonderfully preserved, 80-acre plantation-era estate, originally established in 1864 by plantation owner George N. Wilcox. Comprises a main plantation home, cottages and smaller workers' camp houses. View early-day, plantation-era artifacts, including period furnishings and fixtures, and several personal items, all left more or less untouched, in their original state, reflective of a bygone era. 2-hour guided tours of estate, offered by reservation, at 10 a.m. and 1 p.m., on Mon., Wed., Thurs. Admission: $3.00.

Kauai Lagoons. At the Kauai Marriott, at Kalapaki Beach, Lihue; tours conducted by South Seas Tours, (808) 245-2222/241-6067/(800) 367-2914. The Kauai Lagoons comprise 800 acres of man-made lagoons, dotted with islands inhabited by monkeys, kangaroos, llamas and flamingos. Tours of the lagoons are offered in canopied outrigger canoes; also rides around the lagoons property in 19th-century carriages drawn by Clydesdales. Cost of tours: 1-hour canoe tours, $18.00 adults/$10.00 children; 55-minute Clydesdale-carriage rides, $49.00 adults/$14.00 children.

Kauai Museum. 4428 Rice Street, Lihue; (808) 245-6931. Housed in historic Wilcox Memorial Library Building, dating from the 1930s. Museum features on-going video, "The Story of Kauai," depicting the history of the island, from its geological formation to present day, including the development of Kauai's society and culture. Also on display are several artifacts and exhibits of local historical interest, including such items as stone mortars and pestles from ancient Hawaiian times, sugar plantation-era tools, old photographs, and replicas of a Japanese worker's spartan quarters and a plantation owner's home, with original koa wood furnishings. Museum hours: 9-4.30 Mon.-Fri., 9-1 Sat. Admission fee: $3.00 (children under 18 years, free).

Kilohana Plantation. Located 1½ miles west of Lihue, on Kaumuali'i Highway (50), Puhi; (808) 245-5608. Former sugar plantation estate, dating from the 1930s, situated on 35 acres amid sugarcane fields. Beautifully restored, and furnished in part in Art Deco style. Now houses shops and art galleries, and a courtyard restaurant. Carriage rides and tours of the grounds and nearby cane fields are offered, in carriages drawn by Clydesdales. Open 9.30 a.m.-9.30 p.m., Mon.-Sat., and 9.30 a.m.-5 p.m. on Sundays.

Alakoko (Menehune) Fishpond Overlook. Located on Hulemalu Road (which goes off Wa'apa Road), west of Nawiliwili Harbor. Ancient Hawaiian fishpond, with 5-foot-high and 100-foot-long stone walls, believed to have been built by Kauai's legendary people, the *menehune*, in the course of a single night. The pond is located on the Hule'ia River, on private property; view from the roadside.

Wailua Falls. Located approximately 5 miles north of Lihue, at the end of Ma'alo Road (583), which is off Kuhio Highway (56) just north of Lihue. Picturesque, 80-foot twin falls, quite possibly Hawaii's most photographed and most famous waterfalls, featured in the opening scenes of the TV series, *Fantasy Island*. Picnicking possibilities.

South Shore

Koloa History Center. Koloa Rd. Old Koloa Town. The museum is in fact part of the old Koloa Hotel complex, featuring a courtyard setting, with a recreated, early 1900s barber shop with antique fixtures, and samples of sugarcane, period photographs of Koloa Landing and Old Koloa Town, and several artifacts centered around local history, including such items as a rice thresher, old wooden rakes and saws, antique washing and sewing machines, and a 19th-century Japanese bath tub. Museum hours: 9 a.m.-8 p.m. daily.

Spouting Horn. Just off Lawai Rd., approximately 3 miles west of Poipu. One of Hawaii's best-known and most visited blowholes, where water gushes forth in geyser-like plumes, from a lava tube, when the pressure builds up from sea swells.

National Tropical Botanical Garden. Located at the end of Hailima Rd. (which goes south off Koloa Rd.) in Lawai; (808) 332-7361/332-7324. 186-acre garden, chartered by the U.S. Congress in 1964 and opened to the public in 1971. The botanical garden has lavish displays of tropical plants from throughout the world, and is one of the world's great tropical research gardens, devoted to research and education in tropical plants. The adjacent, 100-acre *Allerton Gardens*, originally established in 1938 by Robert Allerton and his adopted son, John Gregg Allerton, also features tropical plants, including several rare South Pacific plants introduced to Kauai by the Allertons. Also at the Allerton Gardens is the preserved, former home of Queen Emma, wife of King Kamehameha IV. Guided tours are offered of both gardens, at 9 a.m. and 1 p.m.; call ahead for tour reservations. Admission fee: $15.00.

Olu Pua Gardens. Located off Kaumuali'i Hwy. (50), ¹/₂-mile west of Kalaheo; (808) 332-8182. Lush, 12-acre gardens, situated on the former estate of the manager of Kauai Pineapple Plantation. The gardens feature over 5,000 species of tropical plants, trees and flowers. One-hour guided tours of grounds, conducted Mon.-Fri., at 9.30, 10.30, 11.30, 12.30 and 1.30. Admission fee: $10.00.

West Side

Russian Fort Elizabeth State Park. Off Kaumuali'i Hwy. (50), 6¹/₂ miles west of Hanapepe (22¹/₂ miles west of Lihue); (808) 241-3444. 17-acre park, situated on the east bank of the Waimea River. The park has in it the ruins of a Russian fort, originally built between 1815 and 1817, for the Russians, by a German architect, Georg Anton Scheffer, and named for Czarina Elizabeth, wife of Alexander I. A self-guided walk leads past remnants of the fort. Open during daylight hours.

Menehune Ditch. Situated on Menehune Rd. (which goes off Kaumuali'i Hwy.), 1½ miles north of Waimea. One of Kauai's architectural wonders — with its unique construction, featuring flanged and fitted cut-stone bricks, interlocking almost perfectly — attributed to the island's legendary people, the *menehune*. The original ditch was built as an aqueduct, some 24 feet high, to irrigate the *taro* patches in the valley. Only a small portion of the ditch now remains visible.

Kokee Natural History Museum. Situated at the Kokee State Park, on Kokee Rd., 16 miles north of Waimea; (808) 335-9975. Features exhibits of Hawaiian artifacts and indigenous wildlife. Also includes a book section specializing in Hawaiian interest books, and local maps as well as trail maps for the area. Open daily, 10 a.m.-4 p.m. Free admission.

East Side

Fern Grotto. On the Wailua River, inland form Wailua. Popular tourist attraction, and setting for hundreds of weddings each year. Comprises a natural amphitheater-like cave, with huge, overhanging ferns inside it, which also produce some unique acoustics. The Fern Grotto can be reached only by boat, upriver; musicians enliven the boat trips with Hawaiian melodies and sing-along songs along the way. Tour boats depart every half-hour, 8-4 daily; tour cost: $10.00 adults, $5.00 children. For more information on Fern Grotto tours, contact *Smith's Motor Boat Service,* (808) 822-4111, or *Waialeale Boat Tours,* (808) 822-4908.

Kauai Village Museum. Housed in the Kauai Village Market, 4-831 Kuhio Hwy. (56), Waipouli; (808) 822-4904. Small, quaint museum, with informative exhibits and artifacts centered around the Hawaiian way of life. Displays include scale models of a Hawaiian village with thatched dwellings and a heiau with miniature figurines; also ancient Hawaiian stone tools and utensils, and old photographs of interest. Gift shop on premises. Open 10-8 Mon.-Sat., 10-6 Sun. Free admission.

Smith's Tropical Paradise. Located at the Wailua Marina State Park, Wailua; (808) 822-4654. 30-acre cultural and botanical garden, with self-guided paths meandering through beautifully landscaped grounds, amid Kauai's exotic plants, flowers and trees. There are also replicas of Japanese, Filipino and Polynesian villages here, representative of the ethnic diversity of the people of Kauai. Garden luau and international show featured every night, showcasing the entertainment and foods of Tahiti, Hawaii, China, Japan, the Philippines, New Zealand and Samoa. Open 8.30-4 daily. Admission fee: $5.00; luau $43.75 adults/$26.00 children.

Opaeka'a Falls. Situated approximately 2 miles west of Wailua on Kuamoo Rd. (580), which goes off Kuhio Hwy. (50). Scenic 40-foot waterfalls. Picnicking possibilities. Large parking area nearby.

Kamokila Hawaiian Village. Situated at 6060 Kuamoo Road (Hwy. 580), 2 miles west of Wailua; (808) 822-4866. Recreated, ancient Hawaiian village, situated amid taro fields, and comprising a handful of buildings as well as exhibits. Also demonstrations of poi making and mat and skirt weaving. Open 9-4 daily. Admission: $5.00.

Keahua Arboretum. Located on Kuamo'o Rd. (Hwy. 580), some

6½ miles from Kuhio Hwy., inland from Wailua. Lovely, 12-acre preserve, part of the U.S. Forest area. Features more than 20 species of plants; also picnicking, hiking, and swimming possibilities in nearby stream. A half-mile loop trail also leads to a small, natural pool, with a rope swing for swinging out over the water. Open during daylight hours. For more information on the arboretum, call (808) 241-3433.

North Shore

Kilauea Point National Wildlife Refuge. Situated at the northern end of Kilauea Rd. (which goes off Kuhio Hwy.) in Kilauea. Spectacular, 160-acre coastal park, which includes in it Kilauea Point, the northernmost point on the main Hawaiian islands. The refuge is a nesting colony for endangered seabirds, including red-footed boobies, wedge-tailed shearwaters, laysan albatross and great frigate birds, all of which can be seen here, along the rugged coastline. Also, in the winter and spring months, you can see various marine life here, just off the coast, including whales, dolphins, seals and sea turtles. At Kilauea Point there is also an old lighthouse, the *Kilauea Lighthouse*, built in 1913, and still in operation. Park hours: 10-4, Mon.-Fri.; admission: $3.00. Guided, 1-mile hikes conducted Mon.-Thurs., at 10.15 a.m. For reservations for hikes, and more information, call the refuge at (808) 828-1413.

Wai'oli Mission House Museum. Located on Kuhio Hwy. (560), just west of mile marker 3, in Hanalei; (808) 245-3202. Housed in former home of missionaries Abner and Lucy Wilcox, originally built in 1837 and restored in 1921. Features original missionary furnishings from the late 1800s, including antique koa furniture, as well as the original wood-burning stove and bookcases lined with several volumes from Abner Wilcox' collection. Museum hours: 9-3, Tues., Thurs., Sat. Donations accepted.

Haena State Park. Off Kuhio Hwy. (560), approximately 7 miles west of Hanalei. 230-acre park, which includes in it *Haena Beach, Ke'e Beach*, some archaeological sites, and the north shore landmarks, *Waikapalae and Waikanaloa Wet Caves*, located just inside the park, and with their associations to the Hawaiian goddess of fire, Pele. The caves, typically, are deep, dark, and large, with stagnant water. Park open during daylight hours.

Ka'ulu a Paoa Heiau. Located near the western end of Ke'e Beach (which lies in the Haena State Park, off Kuhio Hwy.), and reached by way of a trail, journeying along the shoreline, past the historic Allerton House, then up the hill to the *heiau*. The ancient *heiau* is dedicated to Laka, the Hawaiian goddess of the *hula*, where she, in fact did much of her dancing. Dedicated students of the *hula* still make the pilgrimage to this most sacred shrine of the dance. The site of the heiau also offers good all-round views.

BEACHES

Kauai has some of the loveliest beaches in the Pacific, sandy, secluded, and in idyllic settings. All beaches are public beaches; however, nude bathing at Hawaii's public beaches is prohibited under state law — although some of the beaches continue to be frequented by nudists. Also, a word of caution: several of the beaches on the island are subject to strong under-currents or rip tides, especially in the winter and spring months, making swimming at these beaches, at such times, inadvisable, frequently dangerous; due caution must therefore be exercised at all times when approaching the ocean.

Lihue

Kalapaki Beach. Situated along Kalapaki Bay, at the bottom of Rice St. and Wapa'a Rd., in Lihue; fronts on the Westin Kauai resort. Popular beach, long, wide, sandy, and with gentle waves, offering safe swimming conditions. The beach is also well-liked by sailing and surfing enthusiasts.

Hanama'ulu Beach Park. Located at Hanama'ulu Bay, at the end of Hehi Rd. (which goes off Hanama'ulu Rd., which, in turn, goes off Kuhio Hwy.), approximately 2½ miles northeast of Lihue. The beach, lined with ironwood trees, is a favorite of locals. It has a safe swimming area, especially suited to children, as well as picnicking, camping and fishing possibilities.

Nukoli'i Beach Park. Situated some 3½ miles north of Lihue, bordering on the Wailua Golf Course and the Aston Kauai Beach Villas; reached by way of Kuhio Hwy. (56) north, then Kauai Beach Rd. (which goes off Hwy. 56, roughly a half mile north of the intersection of Hwys. 56 and 51), then right onto an unmarked road (⅓ mile from the Kauai Beach Rd. turnoff), which leads to the beach. Nukoli'i is a narrow, 2-mile-long sandy beach, popular with beachcombers, picnickers, and fishermen. Facilities include restrooms and showers; also ample parking.

South Shore

Poipu Beach Park. Located at the end of Hooni Rd. (which goes off Poipu Beach Rd.), in Poipu. Crescent-shaped, sandy beach, one of the most popular in Kauai; features several pavilions, picnic tables, and showers and restroom facilities. The beach park also incorporates in it a section known as *Baby Beach*, which has a good swimming area, protected by a reef just offshore.

Sheraton Beach. Fronting on the Sheraton Kauai Resort and the Kiahuna Plantation in Poipu; reached by way of a public access road at the end of Hoonani Rd. (which goes off Kapili Rd., which, in turn, goes off Poipu Rd.). Also a crescent-shaped, sandy beach, with good sunbathing, swimming, surfing and windsurfing possibilities. Showers are available at the beach.

Wai'ohai Beach. Situated at the Stouffer's Wai'ohai Beach Resort, just to the west of Poipu Beach Park, and reached by way of short walk from the Poipu Beach Park. This is one of the best snorkeling beaches on the island; it also has a safe swimming area, and is a popular surfing spot. No facilities.

Brennecke Beach. Situated off Hoowili Rd., a quarter mile east of Poipu Beach Park. Small, sandy beach, with a shore break with high energy waves. The beach is a good place for bodysurfing and boogie-boarding. No facilities.

Shipwreck Beach. Situated at the end of Ainako Rd. (which goes off Poipu Rd.), and fronting on the Hyatt Regency in Poipu. A partly-sandy partly-coral beach, where swimming is inadvisable. Well-liked by body-surfers, although the pounding shore break here makes the sport danger-ous for amateurs.

Lawai Beach. Off Lawai Rd., just west of Prince Kuhio Park (which lies 1½ miles west of Poipu). Narrow, roadside beach. Offers fair swimming and snorkeling conditions, but good surfing possibilities, with generally consistent waves — the biggest occurring in the summer months — and a series of surf breaks — "Smokey's," "PK's," "Centers" and "Acid Drop." Showers and restroom facilities at beach.

Mahaulepu Beach. Located approximately 2½ miles northeast of Poipu; reached by way of Poipu Rd. northeastward to the end, then right onto an unmarked cane road that eventually leads to the beach. Long, sandy beach, protected by a coral reef and backed by shallow sand dunes and indigenous vegetation. The beach is quite popular with surfers, windsurfers, and fishermen. No facilities.

West Side

Salt Pond Beach Park. Situated just to the southwest of Hanapepe; reached by way of Lele Rd. (which goes off Kaumuali'i Hwy. (50), just past mile marker 17, west of Hanapepe), then right onto Lokokai Rd. which leads to the beach. The beach is crescent-shaped, and well-liked by area residents. It is protected by a reef just offshore, and offers safe swimming conditions. Beach facilities include picnic tables, pavilions, campsites, and showers and restrooms; also on-duty lifeguard.

Pakala Beach. Located near the village of Pakala, west of Ha-napepe, and reached on Kaumuali'i Hwy. (50), and a dirt trail that goes off the highway, at mile marker 21, passing through a cane field and leading down to the beach. Pakala is a beautiful beach, with superb views of the island of Ni'ihau just offshore. The beach also has locally-famous surf break, known as *Infinities*, with its exceptionally long waves, reaching heights of 8-10 ft. in the summer months. No facilities.

Lucy Wright Beach Park. Located on the western bank of the Waimea River, off Kaumuali'i Hwy. (50), at Waimea. The beach has dark sand, driftwood, and muddy water close in to the shore, due largely to its location adjacent to the mouth of the river. Beach facilities include restrooms and showers; also camping possibilities.

Kekaha Beach Park. Situated at Kekaha, 3 miles west of Waimea, off Kaumuali'i Hwy. (50). Secluded, white-sand beach, backed by shallow sand dunes, which marks the beginning of the 12-mile stretch of beach extending up the coast to the Polihale State Park. The beach, however, is frequented primarily by fishermen and dedicated surfers, and swimming is not advised, due to the strong longshore currents and rip tides.

Majors Bay. Located approximately 7 miles northwest of Kekaha, just off Kaumuali'i Hwy. (50); beach access is generally permitted through the Pacific Missile Range facility. Long, wide, white-sand beach, also popular with fishermen and surfers; offers some of the best surfing conditions on the island. Swimming not encouraged, due to unfavorable ocean currents. No beach facilities.

Polihale State Park. Located roughly a mile north of Majors Bay (8 miles northwest of Kekaha), off Kaumuali'i Hwy. (50), and reached by way of a sign-posted dirt road that goes off the highway, left (or north), some 5 miles, ending at the beach. Polihale is one of Hawaii's most beautiful, secluded, white-sand beaches, 4 miles long and almost 100 yards wide at places, backed by sand dunes, 50-100 ft. high. Offers beachcombing and surfing possibilities; swimming not advised, due to the unsafe ocean conditions. Beach facilities include restrooms and showers; also some camping, by permit.

East Side

Lydgate State Park. Located just south of Wailua, off Kuhio Hwy. (56); reached by way of Leho Dr. (which goes off the highway, east, at mile marker 5), then Nalu Rd. to the very end. Popular family beach, with a breakwater, built from boulders, to protect the beach from a shore break. Offers safe swimming, and picnicking, beachcombing and fishing possibilities. Facilities at the park include picnic tables, restrooms and showers.

Wailua Beach Park. Off Kuhio Hwy. (56), at mile marker 6, in Wailua. Well-liked area beach, half-mile long, and situated near the mouth of the Wailua River. Some swimming possibilities, with on-duty lifeguard; however, exercise due caution when entering the ocean here, as strong rip currents do occur at various points along the beach, especially near the mouth of the river.

Kapa'a Beach Park. Situated at the end of Niu Rd. (which goes off Kuhio Hwy.), in Kapa'a. Narrow, sandy beach; attracts primarily fishermen, as well as some dedicated swimmers.

Kealia Beach. Situated off Kuhio Hwy. (56), at mile marker 10, just north of Kapa'a. Lovely, crescent-shaped sandy beach, lying between two rocky points on the coast. Offers good surfing and bodysurfing, although swimming is unsafe due to the prevailing strong ocean currents here. For swimmers, however, there is a small jetty at the north end of the beach, which offers safe swimming conditions in calm weather. No beach facilities.

Donkey Beach. Located just over 1½ miles north of Kealia Beach (see above), and reached by way of a short walk from the latter. Picturesque, crescent-shaped sandy beach, quite popular with nudists. Swimming, however, is not encouraged here due to the dangerous under-currents. No facilities.

Anahola Beach Park. Situated on Anahola Bay, approximately 3½ miles north of Kapa'a; reached by way of Kuhio Hwy. (56) north, then northeastward onto Kukuihale Rd. at mile marker 13, and right onto a dirt access road, a mile farther, which leads to the beach. Anahola is a long, narrow beach, bordered by shady ironwood trees, and protected by a reef, making it safe for swimming; during high surf conditions, however, dangerous rip tides do occur, with swimming becoming inadvisable. Beach facilities include picnic tables, showers and restrooms.

Moloa'a Bay. Located approximately 7 miles north of Kapa'a, at the end of Moloa'a Rd. (which goes off Koolau Rd, which, in turn, goes off Kuhio Hwy. (56), just north of mile marker 16). Secluded, crescent-shaped beach, rarely visited, offering promising beachcombing and shell-collecting possibilities. Swimming not advised during high surf, when strong under-currents are likely to occur. No beach facilities.

Larsens Beach. Northwest of Moloa'a Bay (see above); reached by way of Koolau Rd. southeast off Kuhio Hwy. (56) near mile marker 20, then off on a dirt road, 1¼ miles farther, which leads to the beach. Larsens is a long, narrow, sandy beach, backed by low sand dunes and shade trees. Popular activities here are beachcombing and fishing; swimming is not recommended, due to the encroaching coral. No facilities.

North Shore

Waiakalua Iki Beach and Waiakalua Nui Beach. Situated east of Kilauea, and reached by way of North Waiakalua Rd. (which goes off Kuhio Hwy.(56), ¾ mile past mile marker 20), then makai — toward the ocean — onto a small dirt road, to the end, from where a short, steep trail leads down to the Waiakalua Iki Beach, a narrow, secluded beach, lined with coral and rock, but with good beachcombing possibilities. Adjoining to the west of Waiakalua Iki Beach, just around a rocky outcropping, is the Waiakalua Nui Beach, a large, sandy beach, at the foot of a deep, lush valley. Waiakalua Nui also has good beachcombing possibilities. Swimming, however, is not encouraged at either of the beaches, due to the coral and unpredictable ocean currents. No facilities.

Kahili Beach (Quarry Beach). Located just northeast of Kilauea, and reached by way of Kilauea Rd., ¼ mile north of the Kong Lung Center, then east onto an unmarked dirt road, which leads, another 1½ miles, directly to the beach. The beach is quite popular with surfers and fishermen. Swimming is not advised in the winter and spring months, and during high surf conditions, due to the dangerous rip tides. No beach facilities.

Kauapea Beach (Secret Beach). North of Kilauea; reached on Kuhio Hwy. (56) west from Kilauea, approximately ½ mile, then right on Kalihiwai Rd., a little way, to a dirt road that heads out north to the beach parking area. This is a long, wide, white-sand beach, especially popular with nudists. Swimming, as with other north shore beaches, is not encouraged here during the winter and spring months, when strong under-currents make it unsafe for the sport. No beach facilities.

Kalihiwai Beach. Located at the end of Kalihiwai Rd. (which goes off Kuhio Hwy.), $\frac{1}{2}$ mile northwest of Kilauea. Wide, sandy beach, bordered by ironwood trees, quite popular with surfers during the winter and spring months. Swimming, however, is inadvisable, due to the strong rip tides and pounding shore break. No facilities.

Anini Beach Park. Off Anini Rd., which goes off the second Kalihiwai Rd., which, in turn, goes off Kuhio Hwy. (56), $\frac{1}{2}$ mile west of mile marker 25, between Kilauea and Princeville. This is a very popular beach, protected from the ocean by a long, wide reef, just offshore. It offers good possibilities for snorkeling, beachcombing, windsurfing, and fishing. Facilities at the park include picnic tables and showers and restrooms.

Sea Lodge Beach. Situated near the Sea Lodge Condominiums in Princeville, and reached by way of Kamehameha Rd. (which goes off Kahaku Rd., the main road leading into Princeville from Kuhio Hwy.) to the very end — at the condominium complex — from where a short walk leads past the condominiums — between blocks B and C and around block A, on the ocean side — following the coastline west to the beach. The beach is part of a small, secluded cove, and offers some swimming possibilities when the ocean is calm; however, strong under-currents do occur, due to the open ocean, and can frequently make the sport unsafe.

Pu'u Poa Beach. Situated at the foot of Princeville Hotel in Princeville, with a public right-of-way at the hotel leading down to the beach. The beach is long, sandy, and protected by a reef, offering good snorkeling possibilities when the ocean is calm.

Hanalei Beach Park. North of Hanalei, on Hanalei Bay; reached by way of Aku Rd. north from Hanalei town, then right onto Weke Rd. which leads to the beach. 2-mile-long beach, quite popular with families. On-duty lifeguard, and picnic tables and restroom facilities.

Black Pot Beach Park. Located at the end of Weke Rd., just past the Hanalei Beach Park (see above). Black Pot is a popular area beach, long, sandy, and offering promising swimming, surfing and windsurfing possibilities. Beach facilities include picnic tables, showers and restrooms.

Wai'oli Beach Park. On Hanalei Bay; reached on He'e Rd., which goes off Weke Rd. The beach is located at an approximate midway point on the bay, and lined with ironwoods. It offers swimming possibilities in calm seas, during the summer months; in winter and spring, the high surf, with its huge, pounding waves, and accompanying rip tides and under-currents, make it unsafe for the sport. Beach facilities includes restrooms and showers.

Waikoko Beach. Located on the west side of Hanalei Bay, off Kuhio Hwy. (560), at mile marker 4. Ironwood-lined beach, with a protective reef and safe swimming area suitable for children. Also offers good snorkeling possibilities when the ocean is calm. No facilities.

Lumahai Beach. 3 miles west of Hanalei; reached by way of Kuhio Hwy. (560) west, $\frac{3}{4}$ mile past mile marker 4, then right onto a dirt trail leading down to the beach. This is one of the loveliest and most famous of Kauai's beaches, which provided the setting for the 1950s classic, *South Pacific*. The white-sand beach is $\frac{3}{4}$ mile long, with some swimming and snorkeling possibilities in the summer months, when the ocean is calm; for the most part, however, the ocean here is unsafe, with dangerous rip tides and under-currents. The west end of the beach —

where the Lumahai River drains into the ocean, and which is reached from the beach parking area, ¾ mile west of mile marker 5 on the Kuhio Hwy. (560) — is popular with experienced bodysurfers, surfers and boogie-boarders. No beach facilities.

Wainiha Beach Park. Situated off Kuhio Hwy. (560), near mile marker 7, in Wainiha. Wainiha means "unfriendly water," and the ocean here is indeed dangerous, with strong rip tides; swimming should not be attempted. No facilities. The beach is frequented primarily by fishermen.

Tunnels Beach. Situated off Kuhio Hwy. (560), ½ mile past mile marker 8 (2 miles west of Wainiha). There are two access trails leading down from the highway to the beach: the first, a mile west of Charo's Restaurant; and the second, two-tenths of a mile farther west from there, with a white access marker located at the turnoff. This is a very popular beach, protected by a large reef and offering a variety of activities, depending on the season and ocean conditions. Excellent diving and snorkeling possibilities during the summer months; and in the winter months, the high surf in the area attracts world-class surfers, to a point beyond the reef, known as *Tunnels*. The beach also has some windsurfing, when the winds are strong enough. No facilities.

Ha'ena Beach Park. Off Kuhio Hwy. (56), near mile marker 9, ¼ mile west of Tunnels Beach. Offers campsites and showers and restroom facilities. Swimming not advised, due to the prevailing strong undercurrents.

Ha'ena State Park (Ke'e Beach). At the end of Kuhio Hwy. (56), at mile marker 10. Excellent swimming and snorkeling beach — in calm seas only — protected from the open ocean by a large reef; during high surf conditions, however, the strong ocean currents can often be dangerous. The beach has a lifeguard, and showers and restroom facilities.

Hanakapiai Beach. 2 miles southwest of Ke'e Beach, reached on the Kalalau Trail. Hanakapiai is a picturesque, white-sand beach in summertime; however, in the winter months, the high surf washes away the beach to expose boulders. Swimming inadvisable due to dangerous under-currents, even in seemingly calm conditions.

Kalalau Beach. Situated at the mouth of the Kalalau Valley, 11 miles southwest of Ke'e Beach; accessed only by way of the rugged Kalalau Trail, or by boat. Long, sandy beach in secluded setting, with a pounding shore break; in the winter and spring months the beach gives way to exposed boulders. Dangerous rip currents, even in calm seas. Swimming not advised; approach ocean with extreme caution.

BEST SNORKELING BEACHES

Poipu Beach Park. Located at the end of Hooni Rd. (which goes off Poipu Beach Rd.), in Poipu. This is one of Kauai's most popular snorkeling beaches, crescent-shaped and with a sandy bottom, offering excellent snorkeling possibilities quite close to the shore, with a variety of marine life.

Lawai Beach. Situated off Lawai Rd., just to the west of Prince Kuhio Park, approximately 11/2 miles from Poipu. Offers good snorkeling in shallow waters, over a lava bed, some 50 yards from the shore. The beach is protected by a coral reef.

Lydgate State Beach Park. Located just south of Wailua, and reached by way of Kuhio Hwy. (56) north from Lihue, then east onto Leho Dr. at mile marker 5, and off onto Nalu Rd. to the very end. Offers an excellent snorkeling area for beginners, protected by a rock wall. Popular with vacationing families.

Anini Beach. Located on the north shore, off Anini Rd., which goes off the second Kalihiwai Rd., which, in turn, goes off Kuhio Hwy. (56), $\frac{1}{2}$ mile past mile marker 25, west of Kilauea. Popular snorkeling beach, ideal for beginners, with a protective coral reef just offshore.

Tunnels Beach. Located one mile west of Charo's Restaurant (west of Hanalei and Wainiha), off Kuhio Hwy. (560), and reached by way of a dirt road that goes off the highway, seaward, to the park. This is one of best places for snorkeling in Hawaii, protected by a coral reef; it offers lava tubes and cracks and crevices in the reef, with a splendid variety of marine life. Snorkeling not recommended in the winter months during ocean swells.

Ke'e Beach. Situated at the end of Kuhio Highway (560), at mile marker 10, in the Ha'ena State Park. This is an excellent snorkeling and swimming beach, protected from the open ocean by a large coral reef, and offering a variety of marine life. Snorkeling not recommended during high surf conditions, when the strong ocean currents can often be dangerous.

HIKING TRAILS

East Side Trails

Wailua Falls Trail. The trailhead is situated off Ma'alo Rd. (which goes off Kuhio Hwy. (56), $3\frac{3}{4}$ miles north of Kapaia (or 4 miles north of Lihue). Strenuous, $\frac{1}{2}$-mile trail; journeys along the south side of the Wailua River to lead to a large, natural pool at the bottom of the Wailua Falls, which has some swimming possibilities.

Nounou Mountain (Sleeping Giant) Trail. There are two trails here, leading to the top of the Nonou Ridge. The first of these, the Westside Trail, begins $\frac{1}{4}$ mile north of mile marker 4 on Kuamo'o Rd. (580) (4 miles inland from Wailua), off Kamalu Rd. (581), in the Wailua Homesteads, and journeys $1\frac{1}{2}$ miles, to the summit; and the other, the Eastside Trail, starts out from Haleilio Rd. (which goes off Kuhio Hwy. 56), just over a mile west from Wailua, then climbs steeply, approximately 2 miles, to the summit. The summit (elevation 1,160 ft.) has good all-round views, and picnicking possibilities.

Keahua Arboretum Trail. The trailhead is located on the south side of Kuamo'o Rd. (580), just across the stream from the Keahua Arboretum — which, in turn, is located some 7 miles west from Wailua, on

Kuamo'o Rd. (which goes off Kuhio Hwy. 56). Easy, ½-mile trail, passing through an area featuring native and introduced tropical plants; there is also a natural pool here, ideal for swimming, roughly 100 yards downstream.

Kuilau Ridge Trail. The trailhead is situated on the north side of Kuamo'o Rd (580), just before reaching Keahua Arboretum (see Keahua Arboretum Trail). Scenic, 2-mile trail, with superb views of the Makaleha Mountains to be enjoyed enroute.

Moalepe Trail. This is also a scenic trail that begins near the intersection of Olohena Rd. (581) — which goes off Kuhio Hwy. (56) — and Waipouli Rd., some 3 miles west from Kapa'a. 2½-mile trail; offers views of the Makaleha Mountains and the ocean farther west.

Na Pali Coast Trails

Kalalau Trail. Begins at Ke'e Beach, at the end of Kuhio Hwy. (560), some 8 miles west of Hanalei. This is one of Kauai's most famous trails, journeying along the rugged and stunning Na Pali Coast, treating hikers to some of the most spectacular coastal scenery along the way. The trail passes by the Hanakapiai Beach and Hanakoa Valley and ends at the Kalalau beach and valley. Strenuous, 11-mile hike; allow at least 6 hours each way.

Hanakapiai Falls Trail. The trail begins at Hanakapiai Stream — reached on the Kalalau Trail, 2 miles southwest of Ke'e Beach — and leads inland, following the stream, to the Hanakapiai Falls in the Hanakapiai Valley. The trail also passes by some ancient stone walls, the ruins of a coffee mill, and a series of waterfalls and natural pools. 1¾ miles each way.

Hanakoa Falls Trail. Also goes off the Kalalau Trail, just west of mile marker 6, and follows the Hanakoa Stream into the Hanakoa Valley and the spectacular, 1,000-foot Hanakoa Falls, cascading into a large pool. ½-mile trail, of moderate difficulty.

Waimea Canyon and Kokee State Park Trails

Iliau Nature Loop Trail. Easy, ½-mile loop trail, begins just before mile marker 9, off Kokee Rd. (550). The trail winds past rare iliau plants, all clearly marked, and vista points with views of the Waimea Canyon.

Kukui Trail. Begins at the Iliau Nature Loop Trail trailhead — just south of mile marker 9 on Kokee Rd. The trail descends some 2,000 feet to the canyon floor and the Waimea River, passing through groves of kukui nut trees along the way. 2½-mile trail.

Koaie Canyon Trail. This trail goes off the Kukui Trail (see above), and journeys alongside the Koaie Stream, on the south side, passing by several natural pools enroute, ideal for swimming. 3-mile trail; should not be attempted when the Waimea River is high.

Canyon Trail. Strenuous, 1½-mile trail. Begins along Halemanu Rd., which goes off Kokee Rd., just north of mile marker 14. Leads to the Waipoo Falls and the Kumuwela Lookout which offers some of the best views of the Waimea Canyon.

Black Pipe Trail. Short, ½-mile trail, connecting the Canyon Trail (see above) to Halemanu Road.

Halemanu-Kokee Trail. This trail also begins along Halemanu Rd., which goes off the main road, Kokee Rd., just north of mile marker 14. The trail offers a self-guided nature walk through koa and lehua forests, abundant in native birds. 1½-mile trail.

Nature Trail. Short loop-trail, passing through small forest area, beginning and ending at the Kokee Natural History Museum on Kokee Road.

Ditch Trail. The trailhead can be reached on either Kumuwela Rd. or Mohihi Rd., roughly 1½ miles from the Kokee State Park Headquarters. Difficult, 3½-mile trail, threading in and out of gulches; superb views enroute, of the inner canyon and its many waterfalls.

Pu'u Ka Ohelo-Berry Flat Trails. Easy, 2-mile loop-trail, which begins just off Mohihi Rd., 1½ miles from park headquarters, and winds through forests of California redwoods, Australian eucalyptus and native koa trees.

Nualolo Trail. The trail begins just west of the park headquarters, off Kokee Rd. (550), and leads through high-altitude forests, before descending some 1,500 feet to a lookout at an elevation of 2,200 feet, directly above Nualolo Valley, which has commanding views of the Na Pali Coast. Strenuous, 4-mile trail.

Nualolo Cliff Trail. A 2-mile trail of moderate difficulty, connecting the Nualolo and Awa'awapuhi trails. Offers scenic views of the Nualolo Valley.

Awa'awapuhi Trail. One of Kokee State Park's most popular trails; begins near mile marker 17 on Kokee Rd. (550), and descends some 1,500 feet to an overlook (elevation 2,500 ft.) with spectacular views of the Awa'awapuhi Valley and Na Pali Coast. 3¼-mile trail.

Kaluapuhi Trail. 2-mile forest trail, beginning ¼ mile northeast of mile marker 17 on Kokee Rd. (550). The trail is especially popular in the summer months, when the wild plums — to be found enroute — ripen.

Pihea Trail. The trail begins at the end of Kokee Rd. (550), at the Pu'u o Kila Lookout, then proceeds along the rim of the Kalalau Valley for about a mile, to Pihea Peak, before descending into the Alakai Swamp, where it intersects both the Alakai Swamp and Kawaikoi Stream trails. 3¾-mile trail, of moderate difficulty.

Alakai Swamp Trail. Strenuous, 3½-mile trail, begins on Mohihi Rd. — a dirt road which may be impassable during heavy rains — near the park headquarters, and leads through Hawaii's largest swamp, containing native rain forests and bogs, ending at the Kilohana Lookout which offers good views of the Wainiha Valley and the Hanalei Bay in the distance.

Kawaikoi Stream Trail. The trailhead is located approximately midway between Kawaikoi Camp and Sugi Grove, along Mohihi Rd. — which goes off Kokee Rd. and which may be impassable in rainy weather. Easy, 3-mile loop-trail; journeys along the Kawaikoi Stream — with several natural pools to be encountered along the way, ideal for swimming — and also passes through some beautiful forest areas.

CAMPGROUNDS

State Park Campgrounds

(For camping permits and information on state park campgrounds, contact the *Department of Land and Natural Resources*, State Office Building, 3060 Eiwa St., Room 306, Lihue, HI 96766; 808-241-3444.)

Hanakapiai Valley. Located 2 miles southwest of Ke'e Beach (which is 8 miles west of Hanalei, at the end of Kuhio Hwy. 560), along the Kalalau Trail. Nearby beach and waterfalls, and several little pools, ideal for swimming.

Hanakoa Valley. Situated high above the ocean, some 4 miles west of the Hanakapiai Valley, on the way to the Kalalau Valley. Idyllic campsites, but with the discomfort of excessive humidity and swarms of mosquitoes, frequently making the conditions unbearable.

Kalalau Valley. Situated approximately 11 miles southwest of Ke'e Beach (which is 8 miles west of Hanalei), at the end of the Kalalau Trail. There are campsites both at the Kalalau Beach and in the valley just inland. Nearby waterfalls, caves, and the broad Kalalau Valley, all well worth exploring. 5-night limit.

Milolii. Remote valley near the western end of the Na Pali Coast, accessible only by small boat in calm seas. Offers some wilderness campsites. Maximum stay, 3 nights.

Polihale State Park. Located on the west side of the island; reached on Kaumuali'i Hwy. (50), some 8 miles northwest from Kekaha, then 5 miles farther northwestward on a sign-posted cane road. The campsites are situated amid small sand dunes; also picnic tables, showers and restroom facilities. Maximum stay, 5 nights.

Kokee State Park. Located on the west side of the island; reached by way of Kaumuali'i Hwy. (50) west to Waimea, then Waimea Canyon Rd. and Kokee Rd. approximately 20 miles northward to the state park. The park as three campgrounds: *Kakalohul Ulhulu Meadow* (located near Kokee Lodge), which has campsites with grills, and restrooms; *Sugi Grove* (situated off Mohihi Rd., which goes east off Kokee Rd., 3 or 4 miles, toward Alakai Swamp), with undeveloped campsites, picnic tables and portable toilets; and *Camp 10* (2 miles past Sugi Grove), which has primarily wilderness campsites, with some picnic tables.

County Park Campgrounds

(For camping permits and information on county park campgrounds, contact the *County of Kauai, Division of Parks and Recreation*, 4193 Hardy Rd., Lihue, HI 96766; 808-241-6670.)

Haena Beach Park. Popular camping area, located on the beach on the north shore, at Haena, some 6½ miles west of Hanalei, off Kuhio Hwy. (560). Offers abundant beach activities, and pavilions, grills, showers and restrooms; swimming not advised.

Anini Beach Park. On Kauai's north shore, between Princeville and

Kilauea. Campsites are situated on Anini Beach, which has a protective reef just offshore, and offers safe swimming as well as good windsurfing possibilities. Pavilions, picnic tables, barbecue grills, showers and restrooms.

Anahola Beach Park. Situated approximately 5 miles north of Kapa'a, near the northeast end of the island, on Anahola Bay, and reached on Kuhio Hwy. (56) and Kukuihale Rd. (which goes off the highway at mile marker 13). The campsites are located on the beach backed by ironwood trees. Facilities include showers and restrooms.

Hanama'ulu Beach Park. Situated at the head of Hanama'ulu Bay, north of Lihue; reached by way of Hanama'ulu Rd. east off Kuhio Hwy. (56), $\frac{1}{3}$ mile, then east again on Hehi Rd., $\frac{1}{2}$ mile, to the beach. Campsites located on beach; facilities include pavilions, picnic tables, barbecue grill, showers and restrooms. Good swimming possibilities.

Niumalu Beach Park. Located near Nawiliwili Harbor in Lihue, at Wapa'a and Hulemalu Rds. Grassy camping area, with pavilions, picnic tables, grills, showers and restrooms.

Salt Pond Beach Park. Situated on Kauai's west side, just to the southwest of Hanapepe, reached by way of Kaumuali'i Hwy. (50) and Lele Rd. Well-liked campsites, located on grassy area on beach. Picnic tables, showers and restroom facilities. Also good swimming possibilities.

Lucy Wright Park. On the west bank of Waimea River, just off Kaumuali'i Hwy. (50), in Waimea. Campsites located near the beach. Restrooms.

GOLF COURSES

Kauai Lagoons Courses. Located adjacent to the Kauai Marriott, off Rice St., Lihue; (808) 241-6000/(800) 634-6400. Offers two 18-hole, par-72, Jack Nicklaus-designed courses — the *Kiele Course* and the *Lagoons Course*, 7,070 yards and 6,942 yards, respectively. Green fees: $145.00 for the Kiele Course, and $100.00 for the Lagoons Course. Pro shop, club rentals, driving range; restaurant and lounge.

Kiahuna Golf Club. 2545 Kiahuna Plantation Dr., Poipu; (808) 742-9595. 18-hole, Robert Trent Jones-designed course; 6,400 yards, par 70. Green fees: $78.00 (including cart), $45.00 after 2 p.m. Facilities include pro shop, club rentals, driving range; also restaurant and bar on premises.

Kukuiolono Golf Course. 854 Pu'u Rd., Kalaheo; (808) 332-9151. 9-hole course with panoramic views; 2,900 yards, par 36. Green fees: $5.00. Pro shop, club rentals, driving range, restaurant.

Poipu Bay Resort Golf Course. 2250 Ainako St., Poipu; (808) 742-8711. 18-hole oceanfront course, designed by Robert Trent Jones, Jr.; par 72, 6,023 yards. Green fees: $100.00 (including cart). Pro shop, club rentals, driving range, restaurant and lounge.

Princeville Resort Golf Courses. At the Princeville Resort, off Kuhio Hwy. (56), Princeville; (808) 826-5000/(800) 826-4400 *Prince*

Course, (808) 826-3580/(800) 826-4400 *Makai Course*. The resort offers two world-class, Robert Trent Jones-designed courses: the 27-hole *Makai Course*, and the newer, 18-hole *Prince Course*. The *Prince Course* is 7,309 yards, par 72; and the *Makai Course* comprises three 9-hole par-36 courses — *Makai Ocean*, which is 3,157 yards; *Makai Lakes*, which is 3,149 yards, and the 3,208-yard *Makai Woods*. Green fees: $90.00 (including cart rental), $65.00 for Princeville Hotel guests. Facilities include pro shop, club rentals, and driving range; also restaurant and lounge.

Wailua Golf Course. 3-5351 Kuhio Hwy., Wailua; (808) 241-6666. 18-hole municipal course; 6,585 yards, par 72. Green fees: $18.00 weekdays, $20.00 weekends, and half price after 3 p.m. Pro shop, driving range, restaurant and cocktail lounge.

TENNIS

Coco Palms Tennis Club. 4-241 Kuhio Hwy., Wailua; (808) 822-4921/(800) 338-1338. Offers 9 courts, including 3 clay courts (2 with lights) and 6 hard courts. Clay court fee: $12.00 per day, $10.00 for hotel guests; hard court fee: $9.00 per day, $7.00 for hotel guests.

Kauai Lagoons Racquet Club. Kalapaki Beach, Lihue; (808) 241-6000/(800) 634-6400. 8 courts available for day use; also pro shop, and lessons. Court fee: $20.00 per hour.

Kiahuna Tennis Club. 2253 Poipu Rd., Poipu; (808) 742-9533. 10 courts for day use. Court fee: $15.00 per day, $75.00 per week. Pro shop and restaurant on premises.

Poipu Kai Resort. 1941 Poipu Rd., Poipu; (808) 742-6464/(800) 777-1700. 8 courts available for day use. Court fee: $6.00 per day. Reservations required.

Princeville Tennis Club. Lieopapa Rd., Princeville; (808) 826-9823. 6 courts. Court fee: $12.00 per day.

Public Tennis Courts. *Lihue Tennis Court,* Hardy St. (next to Kauai War Memorial Convention Hall), Lihue; 2 courts with lights. *Wailua Homestead Park,* Kamalu Rd. (Hwy. 581), between mile markers 4 and 5, in Wailua; 4 courts, with lights. *Wailua Homelots Tennis Courts,* Nonou Rd., Wailua; 4 courts with lights. *Kapa'a Tennis Courts,* cnr. Olohena Rd. and Kahau Rd., Kapa'a; 4 courts with lights. *Koloa Tennis Courts,* Maluhia Rd. (next to fire station), Koloa; 2 courts, with lights. *Kalaheo Tennis Courts,* Pu'uwai Rd. (at the Kalawai Park), Kalaheo; 2 courts with lights. *Hanapepe Public Tennis Courts,* Puolo Rd. (at the Hanapepe Stadium), Hanapepe; 4 courts with lights. *Waimea Tennis Courts,* Ola Rd., Waimea; 4 courts with lights. *Kekaha Tennis Courts,* Alae Rd., Kekaha; 2 courts, with lights.

TOURS

Helicopter Tours

Helicopter tours are especially popular on Kauai — perhaps more than on any other Hawaiian island — with several different companies offering flights over the Waimea Canyon, Na Pali Coast and other parts of the island. Tours originate at either the Lihue Airport in Lihue or the Port Allen Airport at Hanapepe. Typically, tour companies utilize any of three different types of helicopters — the Aero-Star, a 6-seater, with all six seats by the windows, offering good views to all passengers; the Hughes 500, a 4-seater, which also offers window seating to all passengers; and the Bell Jet Ranger, another 4-seater, which, nevertheless, has only three window seats, with one passenger being confined to a center seat and, consequently, lesser views. Tours last anywhere from 30 minutes to 75 minutes, and cost $75-$180 per person.

Helicopter Tour Companies. *Air Kauai,* 4491 Rice St., Suite 2, Lihue, (808) 246-4666/(800) 972-4666; *Bali Hai Helicopter Tours,* Hwy. 50, Hanapepe, (808) 335-3166; *Bruce Needham Helicopters,* Ele'ele Shopping Center, Ele'ele, (808) 335-3115/(800) 359-3057; *Inter-Island Helicopters,* 4510 Hana Rd., Hanapepe, (808) 335-5009/(800) 245-9696; *Island Helicopters,* Lihue Airport, Lihue, (808) 245-8588/(800) 829-5999; *Jack Harter Helicopters,* Lihue Airport, Lihue, (808) 245-3774; *Na Pali Helicopters,* Lihue Airport, Lihue, (808) 245-6959; *Ohana Helicopters,* 3220 Kuhio Hwy., Suite 4, Lihue, (808) 245-3996/(800) 222-6989; *Orchid Helicopters,* Hanapepe, (808) 335-6090; *Pacific Island Helicopters,* Ele'ele Shopping Center, Ele'ele, (808) 335-3115; *Papillon Hawaiian Helicopters,* Lihue Airport, (808) 245-9644, and Princeville Airport, (808) 826-6591/(800) 367-7095; *Safari Helicopter Tours,* Lihue, (808) 246-0136/(800) 326-3356; *South Sea Helicopters,* Lihue, (808) 245-7781/(800) 367-2914; *Will Squyres Helicopters,* 3222 Kuhio Hwy., Lihue, (808) 245-7541/245-8881.

Plane and Glider Tours

Fly Kauai. Lihue; (808) 246-9123. Offers one-hour sightseeing flights over the island, on board a Cessna 206; tour cost: $69.00.

Sightseeing Tours

Grayline Tours. Lihue; (808) 245-3344/(800) 367-2420. Variety of full-day and half-day sightseeing tours — including the Waimea Canyon, Poipu and Spouting Horn, Fern Grotto, Opaeka'a Falls, and the Hanalei area. Tour cost: $35-$50 adults, $28-$40 children.

Kauai Mountain Tours. Lihue; (808) 245-7224/(800) 452-1113.

Offers guided four-wheel-drive tours through Waimea Canyon and Kokee State Park. Tours last 6½ to 7 hours, and are conducted by knowledgeable local residents. Cost of tour: $75.00 per person.

Polynesian Adventure Tours. Lihue; (808) 246-0122. Tours of the Waimea Canyon, Fern Grotto, and the Hanalei Valley and surrounding area. Cost: Waimea Canyon/Fern Grotto tour, $60.00; Hanalei tour, $42.50.

Robert's Hawaii. Lihue Airport; (808) 245-9558. Offers narrated tours of the Waimea Canyon and Hanalei area. Tour cost: Waimea Canyon tour, $25.90; Hanalei tour, $25.90.

Trans Hawaiian Kauai. Lihue; (808) 245-5108. Half-day and full-day tours of Waimea Canyon and Wailua; also tours of Hanalei. Cost of tours: half-day tours, $37.75; full-day tours, $70.00.

Bicycle Tours

Kauai Downhill. Lihue; (808) 245-1774. Offers sunrise bicycle rides down from the Waimea Canyon; continental breakfast included. Tour cost: $60.00 per person.

Outfitters Kauai. Poipu Beach; (808) 742-9667. Guided bicycle tours, including the "Kokee Mountain Bike Ecotour," covering 16 miles of forest backroads. Tour cost: $78.00 per person.

Horseback Riding

CJM Country Stables. Poipu Beach; (808) 742-6096. Scenic ocean rides, ranging from one to three hours. Cost: 1-hour ride, $25.00; 2-hour ride, $45.00; 3-hour ride, $60.00.

Pooku Stables. Hanalei; (808) 826-6777. 1- to 3-hour horseback rides through the Hanalei Valley; also waterfall rides. Cost: $27-$75.

WATER SPORTS

Boat Tours and Snorkeling Excursions

Bluewater Sailing. Kapa'a; (808) 822-0525. Sunset sails on a 42-foot Pearson ketch-rigged yacht; also half-day and full-day trips. Includes snorkeling, swimming and whale-watching. Cost: sunset sail, $75.00; half-day tour, $45.00; full-day excursion, $115.00.

Captain Andy's Sailing Adventures. (808) 822-7833. Sailboat excursions aboard a 46-foot catamaran; also half-day whale-watching and snorkeling excursions, and sunset cruises with complimentary pupus and refreshments. Tour cost: snorkeling and whale-watching excursion,

$65.00 per person; sunset cruise, $35.00 per person.

Captain Sundown's Catamaran Sailing. (808) 826-5585. Sailing excursions on board a 40-foot Hawaiian-style catamaran; includes snorkeling and picnicking at remote beaches, and also some whale watching in season. Tour cost: snorkeling excursion, $65.00; sunset cruise, $40.00.

Captain Zodiac Rafting Expeditions. Hanalei; (808) 826-9371/(800) 422-7824. Sightseeing boat tours of the Na Pali Coast. Excursions include some snorkeling, swimming and picnicking. Tour cost: 3-hour tour, $57.00; 4-hour tour, $75.00; 5-hour tour, $105.00.

Catamaran Kahanu. Hanalei; (808) 828-1124. Four-hour catamaran excursions along the Na Pali Coast, with some snorkeling and a hearty, Hawaiian-style buffet included. Cost: $75.00 per person.

Hanalei Sea Tours. Hanalei; (808) 826-7254/(800) 733-7997. Offers a variety of tours of the Na Pali Coast, on board power catamarans or Zodiac rafts. Some snorkeling included; also snacks and refreshments. Tour cost: $50-$105 per person.

Liko Kauai Cruises. Kekaha; (808) 338-0333. Offers 5-hour snorkeling, troll fishing and sightseeing excursions to the Na Pali Coast, aboard a 34-foot cabin cruiser; includes lunch. Cost: $85.00 per person.

Na Pali Adventures. Hanalei; (808) 826-6804. Sightseeing tours of the Na Pali Coast on board power catamarans; includes some snorkeling along the way. Complimentary snacks and beverages. Tour cost: $85.00 per person.

Paradise Adventure Cruises. Hanalei; (808) 826-9999. Four-hour excursions along the scenic Na Pali Coast, on board a 32-foot catamaran; includes snorkeling and picnic lunch. Tour cost: $75.00 per person.

Smith's Motor Boat Service. Wailua; (808) 822-4111/822-5213/822-3661. 1 1/2-hour narrated boat tours of the Fern Grotto; Hawaiian music on board. Departs every half hour, daily 9-2.30. Cost: $10.00 adults, $5.00 children.

South Seas Kauai Lagoons. At the Kauai Marriott, Lihue; (808) 245-2222/241-6067/(800) 367-2914. 45-minute to 4 $\frac{1}{2}$-hour coastal tours aboard a 38-foot fountain speed boat, departing from Nawiliwili Harbor and Port Allen. Also mahogany launch tours, and 1-hour canoe rides at the Kauai Lagoons. Cost: canoe rides, $18.00 adults/$10.00 children; 45-minute mahogany launch tour, $12.00 adults/$6.00 children; speed boat tours, $29-$79 per person.

Sundancer Cruises. Ele'ele; (808) 335-0110/(800) 359-3057. 5-hour Na Pali Quest Tour on board a 32-foot Australian-built catamaran; includes sightseeing and snorkeling, and a deli buffet-style lunch. Also sunset and whale-watching cruises, and Wet & Wonderful snorkeling excursions along the south shore. Tour cost: Na Pali Quest Tour, $84.00 adults/$74.00 children; Sunset Cruise, $60.00; Wet & Wonderful snorkeling excursion, $59.00; whale watching tour, $59.00.

Waialeale Boat Tours. Wailua; (808) 822-4908. Offers Fern Grotto tours, 2 1/2 miles upriver on the Wailua River; includes narrative and traditional Hawaiian music enroute. Departs every half hour, daily 9-3. Tour cost: $10.00 adults, $5.00 children.

Wayne's World Charter Service. Waimea; (808) 338-1312. Offers 6-hour tours of the Na Pali Coast; includes snorkeling and fishing, and a picnic lunch. Also 4- and 6-hour fishing trips along the island's west coast. Cost: Na Pali Coast tour, $110.00; fishing trips, $85-$110.

Whitney's Boat Cruises. Hanalei; (808) 826-6853. Morning and afternoon tours of the Na Pali Coast on board a 24-foot power catamaran; includes some swimming, and also snorkeling on the morning trips. Complimentary snacks and drinks. Tour cost: morning tour, $70.00 adults, $50.00 children; afternoon tour, $60 adults, $50 children.

Scuba Diving

Scuba diving is a popular recreational sport in Kauai, with several different companies offering introductory scuba dives as well as tank dives for certified divers. Dives are offered both from the shore and from boats. Rates range from $70-$75 for introductory dives, to $65-$85 for tank dives; equipment is generally included.

Scuba Diving Outfitters and Operators. *Aquatic Adventures,* Kapa'a; (808) 822-1434. *Bay Island Water Sports,* Hanalei; (808) 826-7509. *Brennecke's Beach Center,* Poipu; (808) 742-7505. *Bubbles Below Scuba Charters,* Kapa'a; (808) 822-3483. *Dive Kauai Scuba Center,* Kapa'a; (808) 822-0452. *Fathom Five Adventures,* Koloa; (808) 742-6991. *Mana Kai Adventures,* Poipu; (808) 742-9849. *Nitrox Tropical Divers,* Kapa'a; (808) 822-7333/(800) 695-3483. *Ocean Odyssey Dive Shop,* Lihue; (808) 245-8681. *Sea Fun Kauai,* Lihue; (808) 245-6400. *Seasport Divers,* Poipu; (808) 742-7288/742-9303. *Sunrise Diving Adventures,* Kapa'a; (808) 822-7333.

Sportfishing

There are a half-dozen or so companies offering sportfishing charters around Kauai, operating from different parts of the island. Charters, typically, last 4-8 hours, with prices ranging from $90-$120 per person for shared or group charters, to $400-$700 for exclusive trips; rates include all equipment, as well as beverages on the trips. For more information, and reservations, contact any of the following: *Alana Lynn Too Charter Fishing,* Nawiliwili, (808) 245-3866; *Anini Fishing Charter,* Anini, (808) 828-1285; *Gent-Lee Fishing Charters,* Lihue, (808) 245-1853; *Robert McReynolds Fishing Charters,* Anini, (808) 828-1379; *Sea Lure Charters,* (808) 822-5963; *Sport Fishing Kauai,* Koloa, (808) 742-7013; or *True Blue Charters & Ocean Sports,* Lihue, (808) 246-6333.

Kayaking

Island Adventures. Lihue; (808) 245-9662. 2 1/2-hour guided kayak tours of the Huleia Wildlife Refuge and menehune fishpond. Tour cost: $39.00 per person.

Kayak Kauai Outfitters. Hanalei; (808) 826-9844/(800) 437-3507. Offers kayak rentals as well as organized kayak tours, including the Hanalei Wildlife Refuge and Bay Tour, Kapa'a Reef Paddle and Snorkel

Bougainvillea and ti plants

Spouting Horn, on the south shore, erupts in a burst of water and steam

Tour, and the Na Pali Coast Kayak Tour — a full-day adventure, exploring remote beaches and sea caves and journeying close to towering sea cliffs. Cost of tours: Hanalei Wildlife Refuge and Bay Tour, $45.00 per person; Kapa'a Reef Paddle and Snorkel Tour, $45.00 per person; Na Pali Coast Kayak Tour, $105.00 per person (including lunch); and kayak rentals, $48.00 per couple, per day.

Luana of Kauai. Hanalei; (808) 826-9195. Offers 3-hour kayak tours on the Hanalei River, departing at 10.30 a.m. and 1.30 p.m. Cost: $65.00 per person.

Outfitters Kauai. Poipu Beach; (808) 742-9667. Guided sea kayak tours of the lovely Poipu coastline, including a superb view of Spouting Horn along the way, and a visit to a secluded white-sand beach; also full-day Na Pali Kayak Adventure, which includes a 15-mile paddle along the rugged Na Pali coast, from Haena to Polihale Beach. Tour cost: South Shore Sea Kayak Tour, $48.00 per person; Na Pali Kayak Adventure, $115.00 per person.

Paradise River Rentals. At the Kilohana Plantation, Lihue; (808) 245-9580/335-5081/(800) 66-BOATS. Offers kayak rentals as well as self-guided kayak tours of several different island rivers, with topographical maps and instruction in navigation. Also 5-hour guided river trips. Cost: guided tours, $65.00 per person; kayak rentals, $35-$45 per day; power boat rentals for self guided tours, $95-$245 per day.

Pedal & Paddle. Hanalei; (808) 826-9069. All-day, guided kayaking tours along the Na Pali Coast, consisting of a 15-mile paddle from Ke'e Beach to the Polihale State Park. Tour cost: $115.00 per person.

Windsurfing

Hanalei Sailboards. Hanalei; (808) 826-9000. Rentals available, of snorkeling equipment and surfboards and sailboards; daily and weekly rates. Also windsurfing and surfing lessons; cost of lessons: $60.00 for 3-hour windsurfing lesson (including equipment), and $45.00 for 1½-hour surfing lesson (including full-day surfboard rental).

Sea Star Kauai. Kalaheo; (808) 332-8189. Sailboard rentals; $50.00 per day, or $200.00 per week.

Waterskiing

Kauai Water Ski and Surf Company. Kapa'a; (808) 822-3574. 30- and 60-minute waterskiing tows. Cost: 30-minute tow, $45.00; 60-minute tow, $85.00. Reservations required.

RESTAURANTS

(Restaurant prices — based on full course dinner, excluding drinks, tax and tips — are categorized as follows: *Deluxe*, over $30; *Expensive*, $20-$30; *Moderate*, $10-$20; *Inexpensive*, under $10.)

Lihue Area

Barbeque Inn. *Inexpensive-Moderate.* 2982 Kress St., Lihue; (808) 245-2921. Popular local restaurant, serving Japanese and American food. Open for lunch and dinner, Mon.-Sat.

Cafe Portofino. *Moderate-Expensive.* 3501 Rice St., Suite 208, Nawiliwili; (808) 245-2121. Authentic Italian cuisine, featuring a variety of antipastos, homemade pasta, and such house specialties as eggplant parmigiana and scaloppini. Open-air dining, with expansive views of Kalapaki Bay. Open for lunch and dinner. Reservations suggested.

Dani's Restaurant. *Inexpensive.* 4201 Rice St., Lihue; (808) 245-4991. Casual family restaurant, featuring Hawaiian, American and Japanese food, including laulau, omelettes, steak, and teriyaki chicken. Open for breakfast and lunch daily.

Gaylord's at Kilohana. *Moderate.* At the historic Kilohana Plantation, 3-2087 Kaumuali'i Hwy., Puhi; (808) 245-9593. American and Continental cuisine, including a variety of tropical specialties, served in a delightful courtyard setting. Open for lunch and dinner; also Sunday brunch. Reservations recommended.

Hamura's Saimin. *Inexpensive.* 2956 Kress St., Lihue; (808) 245-3271. Popular little restaurant, offering the quintessential "local experience." The favorite dish here is of course Saimen, a bowl of soup and noodles. Open for lunch and dinner.

Ho's Chinese Kitchen. *Inexpensive.* 3-2600 Kaumualii Hwy., Lihue; (808) 245-5255. Offers Mandarin and Szechuan dishes primarily. Open for lunch and dinner daily.

JJ's Broiler. *Inexpensive-Moderate.* At the Anchor Cove Shopping Center, 3416 Rice St., Nawiliwili; (808) 246-4422. Informal. open-air dining, with panoramic views of Kalapaki Bay. Traditional American fare, including homemade soups, sandwiches, salads, steak, seafood and chicken dishes, and freshly-baked bread rolls. Also cocktails. Open for lunch and dinner daily.

Jacaranda Terrace. *Moderate.* At the Kauai Hilton, 4331 Kauai Beach Dr., Lihue; (808) 245-1955, ext. 5566. Casual restaurant, overlooking gardens and pool. Features American and Continental cuisine. Specialties include homemade crab ravioli, stir fry, prime rib, steak and lobster. Open for breakfast, lunch and dinner daily. Reservations suggested.

Kalapaki Beach Hut. *Inexpensive-Moderate.* 3474 Rice St., Lihue; (808) 246-6330. Offers fresh island seafood, and burgers and sandwiches. Informal setting. Open for breakfast, lunch and dinner daily.

Kauai Chop Suey. *Inexpensive.* 3501 Rice St., Nawiliwili; (808) 245-8790. Popular family restaurant, famous for its chop suey. Also other Chinese favorites, such as won ton noodles and sweet and sour pork. Open for lunch and dinner, Tues.-Sun.

Kauai Lagoons Terrace Restaurant. *Moderate.* Kalapaki Beach, Lihue; (808) 241-6080. Garden restaurant, offering lavish buffets; also salads, sandwiches and burgers. Cocktails. Open for lunch daily.

Kun Ja's. *Inexpensive.* 4252 Rice St., Lihue; (808) 245-8792. Authentic, home-style Korean cooking. Specialties include Kalbi ribs, chicken and beef preparations. Open for lunch and dinner daily.

Planter's Prime Rib & Seafood. *Moderate.* Kuhio Hwy., Hanama'ulu; (808) 245-1606. Plantation-style setting. Menu features prime rib, island fish, scampi, lobster tail and roast chicken, as well as freshly-baked garlic bread. Open for dinner. Reservations suggested.

Tip Top Cafe and Bakery. *Inexpensive-Moderate.* 3173 Akahi St., Lihue; (808) 245-2333. Centrally-located, family-style restaurant, serving primarily home-cooked American meals, and freshly baked breads and desserts, and macadamia pancakes. Open for breakfast and lunch daily.

South Shore

Brennecke's Beach Broiler. *Moderate.* 2100 Hoone Rd., Poipu; (808) 742-7588. Beachfront restaurant in outdoor setting, overlooking Poipu Beach. House specialties include kiawe char-broiled fresh island fish, steak, and lobster tail. Also on the menu are chicken and pasta dishes and barbecued ribs. Located directly across from Poipu Beach Park. Lunch and dinner daily. Reservations suggested.

Brick Oven Pizza. *Inexpensive.* 2-2555 Kaumuali'i Hwy., Kalaheo; (808) 332-8561. Family-style pizzeria, featuring a variety of pizzas, including vegetarian pizzas, and homemade sausages and salads. Open for lunch and dinner daily.

Camp House Grill. *Inexpensive.* Cnr. Kaumuali'i Hwy. (50) and Papalina Rd., Kalaheo; (808) 332-9755. Housed in wooden, tin-roofed structure, reminiscent of the plantation days. Offers primarily hamburgers, barbecued chicken and island fish, and freshly-baked, homemade pies. Open for breakfast, lunch and dinner.

Dondero's. *Deluxe.* At the Hyatt Regency Kauai, 1571 Poipu Rd., Poipu; (808) 742-1234, ext. 4900. Elegant Northern Italian restaurant, overlooking Shipwreck Beach. Specialties include fresh pasta, veal and Pacific Northwest salmon. Extensive wine list. Live entertainment. Open for dinner. Reservations required.

House of Seafood. *Moderate-Expensive.* At the Poipu Kai Resort, 1941 Poipu Rd., Poipu; (808) 742-5255. Spacious dining room, surrounded by tropical plants. Good selection of fresh island fish, as well as king crab legs, Hawaiian spiny lobster tail, and New York steak. Cocktail lounge. Open for dinner daily. Reservations recommended.

Ilima Terrace. *Moderate.* At the Hyatt Regency Kauai, 1571 Poipu Rd., Poipu; (808) 742-1234, ext. 4242. Overlooking Shipwreck Beach; open-air dining. Specializes in Pacific Rim cuisine, with emphasis on fresh fish, steak and pasta dishes. Also hearty buffet breakfast and Sunday brunch. Open for breakfast and lunch daily, and brunch on Sundays. Reservations suggested.

Kalaheo Steak House. *Inexpensive-Moderate.* 4444 Papalina Rd., Kalaheo; (808) 332-9780. American fare, served in rustic dining room with hardwood tables. House specialties are teriyaki pork tenderloin and shrimp scampi; also steaks, chicken and fresh seafood. Dinner daily.

Keoki's Paradise. *Moderate.* In the Poipu Shopping Village, Poipu; (808) 742-7534. Tropical, Polynesian setting, amid pools and lush greenery. Favorites here are fresh Hawaiian fish, lobster, steak and ginger chicken. Open for dinner. Reservations suggested.

Koloa Broiler. *Inexpensive.* Koloa Rd., Koloa; (808) 742-9122. Broil-your-own steak, fish and chicken; also salad bar, and baked beans and rice. Cocktails. Open for lunch and dinner.

Lawai Restaurant. *Inexpensive.* 2-3687 Kaumuali'i Hwy., Lawai; (808) 332-9550. Home-style grinds of Filipino, Japanese and American food, including pork adobo, saimen, and hamburgers. Open for breakfast, lunch and dinner.

Pancho & Lefty's Cantina & Restaurante. *Inexpensive-Moderate.* Koloa Town Center, Koloa; (808) 742-7377. Authentic Mexican food, including fajitas, enchiladas and tamales. Family-style restaurant. Open for breakfast, lunch and dinner.

Pizza Bella. *Inexpensive.* In the Poipu Shopping Village, Poipu; (808) 742-9571. California gourmet pizza, and sandwiches, lasagna and pasta dishes. Lunch and dinner daily.

Plantation Garden. *Moderate.* At the Kiahuna Plantation, 2253 Poipu Rd., Poipu; (808) 742-1695. Housed in historical plantation house, in tropical setting, amid lush gardens. Offers Pacific Rim cuisine, featuring crab-stuffed fish, mahi mahi macadamia, and Pacific lobster. Cocktails. Open for dinner. Reservations suggested.

Poipu Bay Bar & Grill. *Expensive-Deluxe.* 2250 Ainako St., Poipu; (808) 742-8888. Serves primarily seafood, steak, prime rib, pasta, chicken, mixed grills, and steak and lobster combination dinners; also sandwiches and salads. Open for breakfast, lunch and dinner daily.

Taisho Restaurant. *Moderate.* 5470 Koloa Rd., Koloa; (808) 742-1838. Traditional Japanese cuisine, featuring fresh seafood, shrimp tempura, and sushi and sashimi. Open for dinner. Reservations suggested.

Tidepools. *Expensive.* At the Hyatt Regency Kauai, 1571 Poipu Rd., Poipu; (808) 742-1234. Well-regarded restaurant, housed in thatched Polynesian huts, surrounded with lagoons, with ocean views. Menu features fresh, broiled fish, and steak, lobster and prime rib. Also cocktails. Dinners daily. Reservations recommended.

West Side

Green Garden Restaurant. *Inexpensive-Moderate.* 13749 Kaumuali'i Hwy., Hanapepe; (808) 335-5422. Delightful garden setting, amid lush, tropical plants. Menu features primarily Continental cuisine, including fresh fish and steak; also homemade lilikoi pies. Cocktails. Open for breakfast, lunch and dinner. Reservations suggested.

The Grove. *Expensive.* Located at the Waimea Plantation Cottages, 9400 Kaumualii Hwy., #367, Waimea; (808) 338-2300. Plantation-style setting, in coconut grove. Menu features multi-cultural Hawaiian specialties, including mahi mahi, Hawaiian seafood stir fry, and bungalow burgers. Also steaks, seafood, chicken, prime rib, and vegetarian lasagna. Open for breakfast, lunch and dinner daily; also Sunday brunch.

Hanapepe Bookstore & Espresso Bar. *Inexpensive.* 3830 Hanapepe Rd., Hanapepe; (808) 335-5011. Housed in historic, 1930s building, with an antique fountain counter that now serves as the espresso bar. Offers homemade scones, freshly-baked croissants and waffles for breakfast, and vegetarian lunches featuring garden burgers and pasta dishes. Also gourmet vegetarian Italian suppers. Live Hawaiian music. Open for breakfast, lunch and dinner. Reservations recommended for dinner.

Kokee Lodge. *Moderate.* Kokee State Park, Waimea; (808) 335-6061. Situated in Kauai's high country, overlooking a beautiful meadow. Menu features American cuisine and island favorites. Also cocktails. Open for breakfast and lunch daily, dinner Fri.-Sat.

Waimea Pizza and Deli. *Inexpensive.* Waimea; (808) 338-0009. Variety of pizza, sandwiches and salads. Also fresh fruit smoothies. Open Mon.-Sat. 11-9, Sun. 11-7.

East Side

Aloha Kauai Pizza. *Inexpensive.* Located in the Coconut Marketplace, 4-484 Kuhio Hwy., Waipouli; (808) 822-4511. Pizza, lasagna, calzone, salads, sandwiches and fresh breads. Open 11 a.m.- 9 p.m. daily.

Bull Shed. *Moderate.* 796 Kuhio Hwy., Waipouli; (808) 822-3791. Oceanview restaurant, featuring fresh seafood, chicken, steak, lobster, and rack of lamb served in traditional American or Polynesian style. Salad bar. Open for dinner. Reservations recommended.

Buzz's Steak & Lobster. *Moderate.* At the Coconut Marketplace, 484 Kuhio Hwy., Waipouli; (808) 822-0041. Polynesian-decor steak house. Offers a variety of steaks, and fresh island seafood. House specialties include deep-fried calamari, and Seafood Brochette. Entertainment. Open for lunch and dinner daily. Reservations.

Flying Lobster. *Expensive-Deluxe.* Located in the Kauai Coconut Beach Resort at the Coconut Marketplace, 484 Kuhio Hwy., Kapaa; (808) 822-3455. Well-regarded seafood restaurant, specializing in fresh lobster and steak and lobster combination dinners. Live entertainment and dancing. Open for dinner. Reservations recommended.

Ginger's Grille. *Inexpensive-Moderate.* 4-831 Kuhio Hwy., Waipouli; (808) 822-5557. American fare primarily, including steaks, chicken and seafood salads. Lunch and dinner daily.

Hanama'ulu Restaurant & Tea House. *Moderate.* 3-4291 Kuhio Hwy., Hanama'ulu; (808) 245-2511. Delightful setting, amid Japanese gardens and ponds. Offers primarily Japanese and Chinese cuisine, including tempura, sushi, chop suey, and beef broccoli. Private tea rooms available. Open for lunch and dinner. Reservations suggested.

Jolly Roger. *Moderate.* At the Coconut Plantation, Waipouli; (808) 822-3451. American and Oriental cuisine. Favorites here are steak, stir fry, fresh fish, Polynesian-style chicken, and shrimp platters. Open for breakfast, lunch and dinner. Reservations.

Kapa'a Fish & Chowder House. *Moderate.* 4-1639 Kuhio Hwy., Kapa'a; (808) 822-7488. Established fish and steak house, decorated with fish nets and other fishing items. Specializes in fresh island fish, as well as char-broiled lobster tails and New York steak, and Cajun shrimp and seafood fettucini. Open for lunch and dinner daily. Reservations suggested.

King and I. *Moderate.* 4-901 Kuhio Hwy., Waipouli; (808) 822-1642. Authentic Thai cuisine. Specialties include sah-teh and fried calamari, and chicken or fresh fish curries; also daily vegetarian specials. Open for dinner. Reservations suggested.

Kintaro Japanese Restaurant. *Moderate.* 4-370 Kuhio Hwy., Wailua; (808) 822-3341. Japanese cuisine, featuring Teppan-style dinners, with chicken teriyaki, lobster tail, and filet mignon; also complete sushi bar. Traditional Japanese decor. Dinner daily. Reservations recommended.

Kountry Kitchen. *Inexpensive.* 1485 Kuhio Hwy., Kapa'a; (808) 822-3511. Home-style American eatery, serving a variety of omelettes, banana pancakes, eggs, steak, pork chops, fresh fish, hamburgers and salads. Open for breakfast, lunch and dinner.

Lagoon Dining Room. *Moderate.* At the Coco Palms Resort, 4-241 Kuhio Hwy., Wailua; (808) 822-4921. Continental cuisine. Menu features New York steak, fresh fish, lobster, and prime rib. Outdoor, Polynesian setting; overlooking lagoons and coconut grove. Breakfast, lunch and dinner daily. Reservations recommended.

Norberto's El Cafe. *Inexpensive-Moderate.* 4-1373 Kuhio Hwy., Kapa'a; (808) 822-3362. Traditional Mexican food, including meat and vegetarian enchiladas grande, burritos and fajitas. Complimentary nachos with fresh, hot salsa. Spanish decor. Open for dinner daily.

Olympic Cafe. *Inexpensive.* 1387 Kuhio Hwy., Kapa'a; (808) 822-5731. Casual cafe, serving Japanese and American food, including chicken katsu, shrimp tempura, oxtail soup, and American-style, grilled island fish and burgers. Open for breakfast, lunch and dinner.

Ono Family Restaurant. *Inexpensive.* 4-1292 Kuhio Hwy., Kapa'a; (808) 822-1710. American and island specialties — sandwiches, burgers, top sirloin, barbecued ribs, buffalo cube steak, mahi mahi, and shrimp plates. Open for breakfast, lunch and dinner daily.

Pacific Cafe. *Moderate-Expensive.* 4-831 Kuhio Hwy., Suite 220, Waipouli; (808) 822-0013. Contemporary setting. Specializing in Pacific Rim cuisine with a European flare. Menu features fresh island fish cooked over a wood-burning grill, pasta, sirloin steak, and roast Chinese duck, served with an array of unique sauces. Open for dinner. Reservations recommended.

Panda Garden Chinese Restaurant. *Inexpensive.* 4-831 Kuhio Hwy., Waipouli; (808) 822-0092. Authentic Chinese cuisine, with emphasis on Szechuan and Cantonese dishes. Lunch and dinner daily.

Paradise Chicken-N-Ribs. *Moderate.* 484 Kuhio Hwy., Waipouli; (808) 822-2505. Serves primarily charbroiled chicken and ribs, and soups, sandwiches and salads. Open for lunch and dinner daily.

Sizzler. *Inexpensive-Moderate.* 4361 Kuhio Hwy., Waipouli; (808) 822-7404. Extensive soup, salad and pasta bar; also some seafood, chicken and steak entrees. Open daily 6 a.m. - 10 p.m.

Wailua Marina Restaurant. *Moderate.* Located in the Wailua River State Park, Wailua; (808) 822-4311. Steaks and seafood, including Hawaiian spiny lobster tail and char-broiled mahi mahi, and barbecued ribs. Outdoor dining, on lanai overlooking Wailua River. Breakfast, lunch and dinner daily. Reservations suggested.

Wild Palms Bistro. *Expensive.* 4-484 Kuhio Hwy., Waipouli; (808) 822-1533. Features steaks, seafood, salads and pasta. Specialties include crab burgers, shish kebab, and steak and lobster combination plates; also some vegetarian dishes. Open for lunch and dinner daily. Reservations recommended.

North Shore

Bali Hai. *Moderate-Expensive.* At the Hanalei Bay Resort, 5380 Honoiki Rd., Princeville; (808) 826-6522. Splendid ocean and mountain views. Specializes in Pacific Rim cuisine, featuring fresh fish, baked salmon, barbecued Thai shrimp, filet mignon and lamb chops. Nightly entertainment; cocktails. Open for breakfast, lunch and dinner. Reservations recommended.

Cafe Di Amici. *Moderate-Expensive.* 2484 Keneke St., Kilauea; (808) 828-1388. Italian restaurant, serving traditional Italian food, including a variety of pasta dishes with an assortment of homemade sauces; also veal piccata, scampi and saltimbocca. Good selection of Italian wines. Open for lunch and dinner. Reservations suggested.

Cafe Hanalei. *Moderate-Expensive.* At the Princeville Hotel, 5520 Kahako Rd., Princeville; (808) 826-2760. Specializing in Pacific rim cuisine. Also offers extensive Thai and seafood buffets. Open for breakfast, lunch and dinner daily, and Sunday brunch.

Charo's. *Moderate.* 5-7132 Kuhio Hwy., Haena; (808) 826-6422. Well-known north shore restaurant, in tropical setting, overlooking the Pacific Ocean; owned by celebrity entertainer Charo. Offers Mexican and Continental dishes primarily. Also entertainment. Open for lunch and dinner. Reservations suggested.

Chuck's Steak House. *Moderate.* Princeville Shopping Center, Kuhio Hwy., Princeville; (808) 826-6211. Fresh fish, lobster, prime rib and top sirloin. Informal setting. Lunch and dinner daily. Reservations recommended.

Hanalei Gourmet. *Inexpensive-Moderate.* 5-5161 Kuhio Hwy., Hanalei; (808) 826-2524. Deli-style sandwiches, served on freshly-baked breads. Also fresh fish, homemade lasagna and pasta dishes. Tropical bar; live entertainment, Tues.-Sat. Open for breakfast, lunch and dinner.

Hanalei Dolphin. *Moderate.* Hanalei; (808) 826-6113. Outdoor setting, in Polynesian atmosphere; overlooking Hanalei River. Menu features fresh fish, abalone, tenderloin steak, buffalo steak and chicken. Also cocktails. Open for dinner. Reservations suggested.

La Cascata. *Moderate-Expensive.* At the Princeville Hotel, 5520 Ka Haku Rd., Princeville; (808) 826-2761. Intimate dining room, with classic Italian decor, overlooking Hanalei Bay and Bali Hai. House specialties include oven-baked sea bass, veal scallopini, and grilled sirloin. Open for dinner; also Sunday brunch. Reservations recommended.

Pizza Hanalei. *Inexpensive.* Ching Young Village Shopping Ctr., Hanalei; (808) 826-9494. Wide selection of pizzas, with homemade whole-wheat or white-flour crust. Also lasagna, salads, and garlic bread. Lunch and dinner daily.

Shell House. *Moderate.* Cnr. Kuhio Hwy. and Aku Rd., Hanalei;

(808) 826-9301. Well-regarded restaurant, situated in the heart of Hanalei. Menu features fresh island fish, steaks, prime rib, chicken and pasta dishes, salads, burgers, homemade clam chowder, and freshly-baked pies. Open for breakfast, lunch and dinner. Reservations recommended.

Tahiti Nui. *Moderate.* Kuhio Hwy., Hanalei; (808) 826-6277. American and Thai cuisine, served in Polynesian setting. Specialties include fresh island fish, chicken curry, and family-style calamari. Luaus Wednesdays and Fridays. Open for lunch and dinner daily. Reservations suggested.

LUAUS

Kauai Coconut Beach Hotel. Kuhio Hwy. (56), Wailua; (808) 822-3455. Extravagant, authentic presentation, with traditional Hawaiian food, music and dance. Luaus begin at 6.15 p.m., Tues.-Sun. Cost: $45.00 per person. Reservations recommended.

Smith's Tropical Paradise. At the Wailua Marina, Wailua; (808) 822-4654. Popular Polynesian show, in beautiful, tropical setting. Features authentic Hawaiian and Polynesian foods. Begins at 6 p.m., Mon.-Fri. Cost: $45.00 per person. Reservations suggested.

Tahiti Nui. Cnr. Kuhio Hwy. (560) and Aku Rd., Hanalei; (808) 826-6277. Traditional luau, with authentic Hawaiian food, and entertainment. Luaus begin at 6.30 p.m., Wednesdays and Fridays. Cost: $35.00 per person. Reservations suggested.

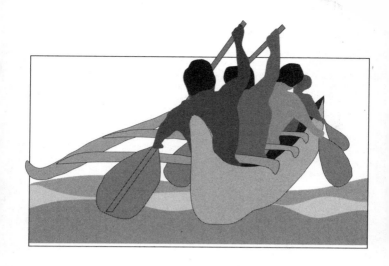

NI'IHAU

"The Forbidden Isle"

Ni'ihau is Hawaii's "Forbidden Isle" — forbidden, that is, to visitors as well as Hawaiians who are not resident on Ni'ihau itself. The island is privately owned, by the Robinson family, descendants of Elizabeth Sinclair, a Scottish woman, who, in 1864, while traveling from New Zealand with her family, came upon Ni'ihau and purchased the island from King Kamehameha V, for a reported $10,000, to raise sheep and cattle. Cattle ranching is still the principal industry on the island, and the Robinsons, like Elizabeth Sinclair before them, continue the tradition of excluding outsiders from the island, preserving it as the last vestige of the Hawaiian way of life.

Ni'ihau is approximately 72 square miles in area — 18 miles long and 6 miles wide — the smallest of the main Hawaiian islands, situated some 17½ miles west-southwest of Kauai. It comprises, for the most part, flat, arid land, with an average annual rainfall of only 25-30 inches. The highest point on the island is Paniau, with an elevation of 1,281 feet. Besides which, the island has on it the largest lake in the state of Hawaii, Halali'i, covering roughly 850 acres, and filled, quite ironically, with rain water.

The population of Ni'ihau — all of 220 — is concentrated largely on the west shore of the island, in the small village of Pu'uwai. The island has no electricity — refrigerators and television sets are powered by generators — or plumbing or telephones, and the island's catchment system is used to collect

T

N

K

PACIFIC

OCEAN

Kaunanui Pt.

Kalanaei Pt.

Lake
Loe

Kaumuhonu

Puuwai

Kiekie

Pakaua Pt.

Halulu
Lake

Nonopapa

Nonopapa
Lake

Halalii
Lake

Pooneone P

Makahuena Pt.

KAWAEWAE

Alieiki
Lake

Oiamoi Pt.

Kamalino

Kowahi Pt.

Pahau Pt.

Leahi Pt.

KAWAIHOA
PENINSULA

Kaumuhonu
Bay

Kawaihoa Pt.

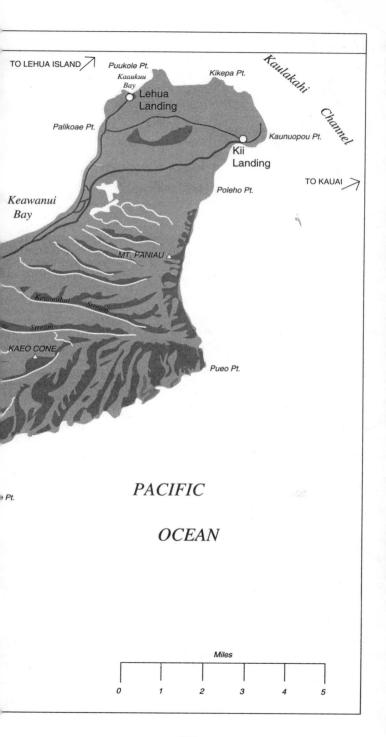

TO LEHUA ISLAND

Puukole Pt.

Kaaukuu Bay

Lehua Landing

Palikoae Pt.

Kikepa Pt.

Kaulakahi

Channel

Kaunuopou Pt.

Kii Landing

TO KAUAI

Poleho Pt.

Keawanui Bay

MT. PANIAU △

Keawanui Stream

Stream

KAEO CONE
△

Pueo Pt.

Pt.

PACIFIC

OCEAN

Miles

0   1   2   3   4   5

water.

The primary language spoken on Ni'ihau is Hawaiian, with English as the secondary language. The island, besides, has one school, up to the eighth grade level, beyond which students must transfer to a school on Kauai to continue their education.

Ni'ihau's residents are employed either on the island's cattle ranch or on the Gay & Robinson sugar plantation at Makaweli, on the west shore of Kauai. Interestingly, island residents are permitted to come and go, to and from the island, at their choosing; however, once they leave the island as their place of residence, they may only return to visit family members still residing on the island.

Ni'ihau is of course famous for its sea shells, unique and beautiful, and found nowhere else in the Pacific, other than here. The shells are used to make leis, among the most treasured —and, yes, expensive — in Hawaii. The island's hand-woven mats are also highly regarded, both for their craftsmanship and design.

Ni'ihau, we might add, is also notable as the site of a particularly memorable incident during World War II, in which a Japanese pilot crash landed his plane on the island — on the day of the attack on Pearl Harbor — and briefly terrorized the island's inhabitants, brandishing his pistol and machine-gun, and shooting, during a scuffle, a young Hawaiian named Ben Kanahele. Kanahele, however, we are told, bloodied and enraged, picked up the pilot bodily and smashed his head into a stone wall, thus killing the Japanese. Kanahele was subsequently decorated for his bravery in the short-lived "Battle of Ni'ihau," and the incident gave rise to the popular Hawaiian phrase, "Never shoot a Hawaiian three times, for that's when he'll get mad at you!"

TOURING NI'IHAU

The best — and only — way to see Ni'ihau, the "Forbidden Isle," is on an organized helicopter tour, offered by the Robinson family interests.

The tours, typically, last 3 hours, covering much of the island — with the notable exception of the village of Pu'uwai — and include a 20-minute recess on the south shore and a 1-hour stop on the north shore. Refreshments are provided at the stops and enroute, and there are some good beachcombing possibilities on the island's beaches. Cost of tour: $200.00. For reservations and more information, contact *Ni'ihau Helicopters*, Makaweli, at (808) 335-3500.

HAWAIIAN GLOSSARY

The Hawaiian language, in its simplicity, contains only seven consonants — H, K, L, M, N, P, W — and five vowels — A, E, I, O and U. All words — and syllables — end in a vowel, and all syllables begin with a consonant. The vowels, typically, are each pronounced separately — i.e., *a'a* is pronounced "ah-ah," and *e'e* is pronounced "ay-ay"; the only exceptions are the diphthong double vowels — *ai,* pronounced "eye," and *au,* pronounced "ow." The consonants, on the other hand, are never doubled.

Hawaiian consonants are pronounced similar to those in English, with the notable exception of W, which is sometimes pronounced as "V," when it begins the last syllable of the word. Hawaiian vowels are pronounced as follows: A - "uh," as in among; E - "ay," as in day; I - "ee," as in deep; O - "oh," as in no; U - "oo," as in blue.

For travellers to the Hawaiian islands, the following is a glossary of some commonly used words in the Hawaiian language.

a'a — rough, crumbling lava.
ae — yes.
ahi — tuna fish.
ahupua'a — pie-shaped land division, extending from the mountains to the sea.
aikane — friend.
alanui — road, or path.
ali'i — a Hawaiian chief or nobleman.
aloha — love, or affection; traditional Hawaiian greeting, meaning both welcome and farewell.
anu — cold, cool.
a'ole — no.
auwe — alas!
awawa — valley.

hala — the pandanus tree, the leaves of which are used to make baskets and mats.
hale — house.
hale pule — church; house of worship.
hana — work.
hahana — hot, warm.
haole — foreigner; frequently used to refer to a Caucasian.
hapa — half, as in *hapa-haole,* or half Caucasian.
haupia — coconut cream pudding, often served at a luau.
heiau — an ancient Hawaiian place of worship; shrine, temple.
holoholo — to go for a walk; also to ride or sail.
honi — a kiss; also, to kiss.
hui — a group, society, or assembly of people.
hukilau — a communal fishing party, in which everyone helps pull in the fishing nets.

GLOSSARY

hula — traditional Hawaiian dance of storytelling.
imu — underground oven, used for roasting pigs for luaus.
ipo — sweetheart, or lover.

ka'ahele — a tour.
ka'ao — legend.
kahuna — priest, minister, sorcerer, prophet.
kai — the sea.
kakahiaka — morning.
kama'aina — native-born, or local.
kanaka — man, usually of Hawaiian descent.
kane — male, husband.
kapu — taboo, forbidden; derived from the Tongan word, *tabu*.
keiki — child; a male child is known as *keikikane*, and a female
    child, *keikiwahine*.
kiawe — Algaroba tree, with fern-like leaves and sharp, long
    thorns, usually found in dry areas near the coast. Kiawe
    wood is used to make charcoal for fuel. The tree was
    introduced to Hawaii in the 1820s.
koa — native Hawaiian tree, prized for its wood which was used
    by early Hawaiians to craft canoes, spears and surfboards.
    Koa wood is now used to make fine furniture.
kokua — help.
kona — leeward side of island; frequently used to describe
    storms and winds, such as *kona* storm or *kona* wind. Also,
    south.
ko'olau — windward side of island.
kukui — Candlenut tree, characteristic in its yellow and green
    foliage, generally found in the valleys. Kukui nuts are also
    used in leis. Kukui is Hawaii's state tree.
kuleana — home site, or homestead; also responsibility, or
    one's business.
kupuna — grandparent.

lamalama — torch fishing
lanai — porch, veranda, balcony.
lani — the sky, or heaven
laulau — wrapped package; generally used to describe bundles
    of pork, fish or beef, served with taro shoots, wrapped in *ti*
    or banana leaves, and steamed.
lei — garland, wreath, or necklace of flowers.
lilikoi — passion fruit.
limu — seaweed.
luau — traditional Hawaiian feast.

mahalo — thanks, or thank you.
mahimahi — dolphin.
maile — native vine with shiny, fragrant leaves used in leis.
makahiki hou — New Year; *hauoli makahiki hou*, Happy New
    Year.
make — to die, or dead.

makai — toward the ocean, or seaward.
malihini — stranger, newcomer.
mana — supernatural power.
manu — bird.
mauka — toward the mountain, or inland.
mauna — mountain.
mele — song, chant.
menehune — Hawaii's legendary little people, ingenious and hardworking, who worked only at night, building fishponds, heiaus, irrigation ditches and roads, many of which remain today.
moana — the ocean; open sea.
mo'o — lizard, dragon, serpent.
mu'umu'u — long, loose, traditional Hawaiian dress.

nani — beautiful.
nui — big.

ohana — family.
ono — delicious.

pakalolo — marijuana.
palapala — book; also printing.
pali — cliff; also plural, cliffs.
paniolo — Hawaiian cowboy.
pau — finished, all done.
poi — a purplish paste made from pounded and cooked taro roots; staple of Hawaiian diet.
puka — hole, opening.
pupu — appetizer, snack, hors d'oeuvre.
pupule — crazy; insane.

tapa — cloth made from beaten bark, often used in Hawaiian clothing.
taro — broad-leafed plant with starch root, used to make poi; staff of life of early Hawaiians, introduced to the islands by the first Polynesians.
ti — broad-leafed plant, brought to Hawaii by early Polynesian immigrants. *Ti* leaves are used for wrapping food as well as offerings to the gods.

waha — mouth; *waha nui*, a big mouth.
wahine — female, woman, wife.
wai — fresh water.
wiki — to hurry; *wikiwiki*, hurry up.

Hibiscus

Anthurium

Bird of Paradise

Torch Ginger

White Ginger

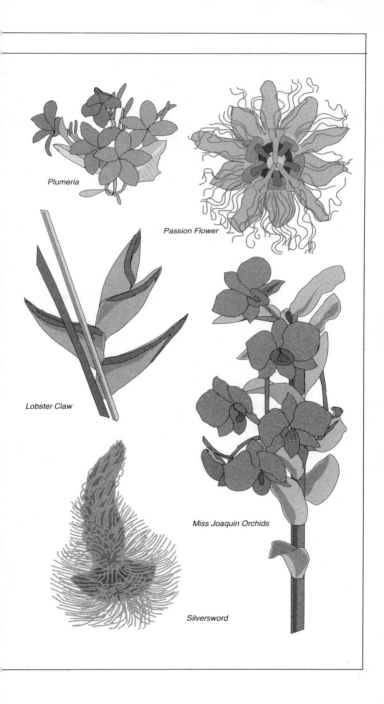

Plumeria

Passion Flower

Lobster Claw

Miss Joaquin Orchids

Silversword

113

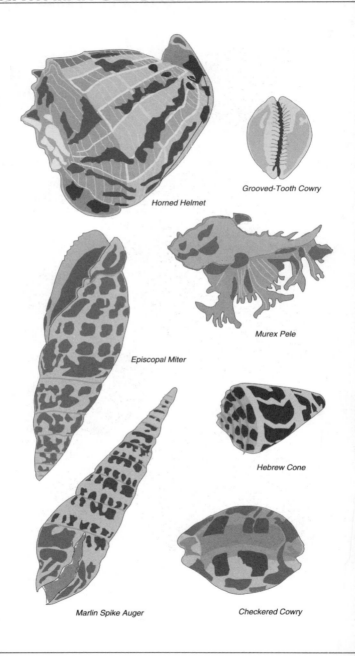

Horned Helmet

Grooved-Tooth Cowry

Episcopal Miter

Murex Pele

Hebrew Cone

Marlin Spike Auger

Checkered Cowry

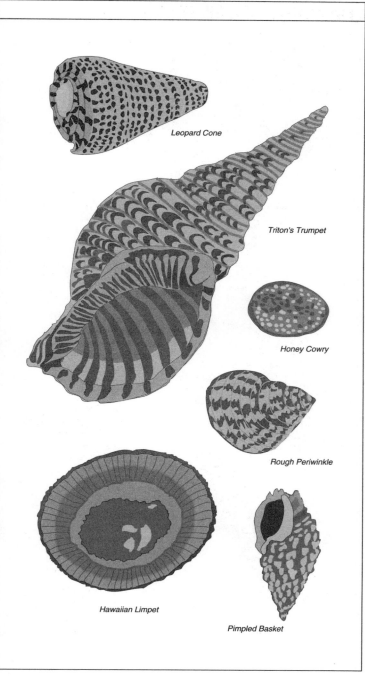

Leopard Cone

Triton's Trumpet

Honey Cowry

Rough Periwinkle

Hawaiian Limpet

Pimpled Basket

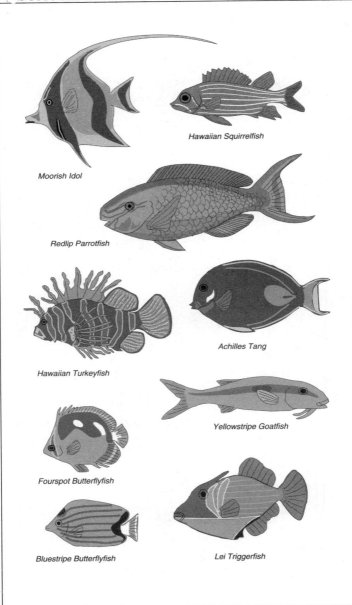

Moorish Idol

Hawaiian Squirrelfish

Redlip Parrotfish

Hawaiian Turkeyfish

Achilles Tang

Yellowstripe Goatfish

Fourspot Butterflyfish

Bluestripe Butterflyfish

Lei Triggerfish

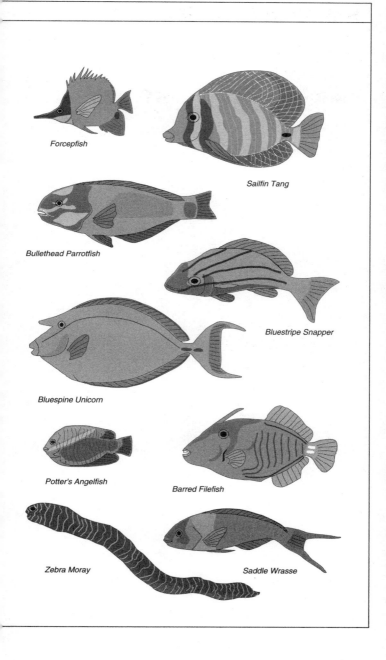

Forcepfish

Sailfin Tang

Bullethead Parrotfish

Bluestripe Snapper

Bluespine Unicorn

Potter's Angelfish

Barred Filefish

Zebra Moray

Saddle Wrasse

117

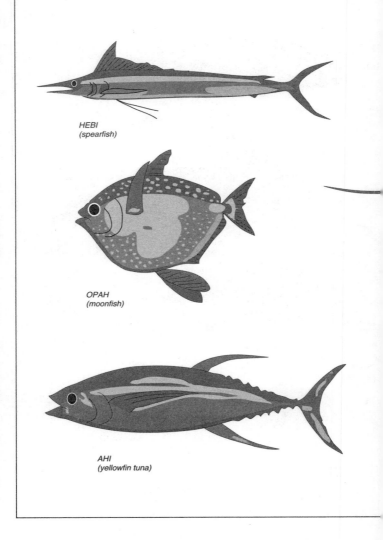

HEBI
(spearfish)

OPAH
(moonfish)

AHI
(yellowfin tuna)

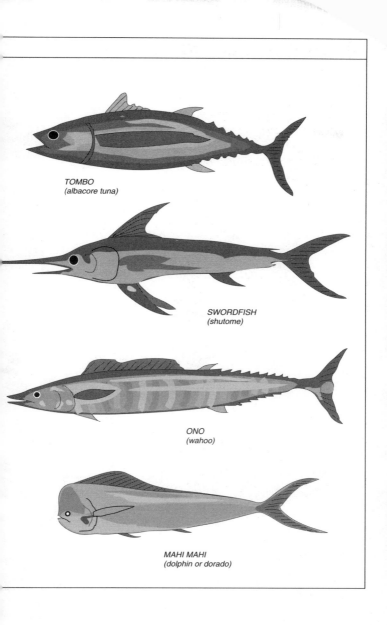

TOMBO
(albacore tuna)

SWORDFISH
(shutome)

ONO
(wahoo)

MAHI MAHI
(dolphin or dorado)

Plumeria Lei

Maunaloa Lei

Maile Lei

Lei Mokihana

Vanda Orchid Lei

Peacock Feathers Lei

Pheasant Feathers Lei

Niihau Shells Lei

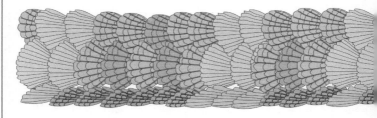

Lei Olepe

Shell Lei

ERS)

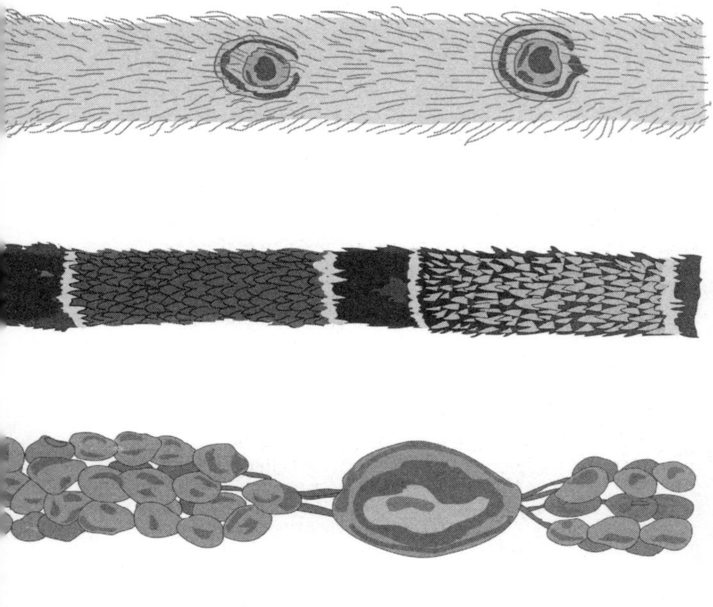

INDEX

INDEX